Engineering Legitimacy

Iva Petkova

Engineering Legitimacy

How Institutional Entrepreneurs in E-Commerce
Bring Fashion Companies into the Digital Age

Iva Petkova
Ringling College of Art and Design
Sarasota, FL, USA

ISBN 978-3-030-08079-2   ISBN 978-3-319-90707-9   (eBook)
https://doi.org/10.1007/978-3-319-90707-9

Cover credit: Designed by Akihiro Nakayama

Printed on acid-free paper

This Palgrave Macmillan imprint is published by the registered company Springer International Publishing AG part of Springer Nature
The registered company address is: Gewerbestrasse 11, 6330 Cham, Switzerland

In memory of my Grandmother, Rumi

PREFACE

This book arose as a subject of my long-term ethnography, hailing from Columbia University's Sociology Department all the way to London, Milan, Paris, and back. I discovered the topic while walking the National Retail Federation's Big Show at the Javits Center in New York in 2010. My main scholarly interest was rather clear: a fascination with empirical worlds at the threshold of technology, creative cultural industries, and entrepreneurship. My goal while there was to search for innovations and unique developments in technology and culture, particularly in fields surrounding the fashion industry. In my ethnography notes post-NRF, I had feverishly scribbled: "the most difficult times often spot innovation. Retailers and technology companies are embracing the need for new technology, new paradigms, new culture..." e-commerce was the big tech hike. But, while companies of every industry embraced the migration of their businesses and brands online, the numerous fashion company representatives I sought out, were not particularly in on this memo. Meetings featuring fashion professionals discussed familiar topics: trend research, product design, development, and their further automation. The big reveal came in a flash (as these always tend to), during a meeting of trend experts in fashion, who seemed to offer to my attention more insight about fashion industry's ritualism and conformity than they (or Merton himself) would have known: "Classic definition of fashion is a reflection of the society we live in", one of these long-time industry experts intoned, "and society is so fractured that people in forecasting, manufacturing, merchandising, or selling haven't yet understood that the old yardstick of mainstream mentality no longer works. You could predicate your plans based upon your simple equation, but we have a hundred different rivulets of fashion, moving in different directions. Is trending, for instance, *still* trendy?"

These sage voices of (mild) dissent led me to pursue two interrelated avenues for my research: were there any fashion companies that passionately pursued new technology developments, specifically with regard to repositioning their brands, businesses, organizations, and cultures online? Correspondingly, were there any high-tech Internet entrepreneurs, which sought to persuade this shift in "consciousness" in incumbent fashion firms? And if they did, and could, how were they achieving this unfathomable feat? These musings later transformed into serious scholarly pursuit addressing some long-standing question marks in the sociology of organizations. How do emerging institutional entrepreneurs, often outsiders to institutionalized organizations in creative culture industries, legitimize their practice with incumbents in such creative fields? And, how can rhetorically driven incumbents in the fashion industry risk aligning their identity with the technology-driven identity of e-commerce and social commerce entrepreneurs?

The reader probably suspects that John Meyer and Brian Rowan had allured me as a scholar with their initial hypotheses on myth and ceremony in institutionalized organizations. Mark Suchman, later, enticed me to answer these questions by looking at legitimation processes. And, Woody Powell recently cemented the deal for me, by having "sent" a scholarly invitation to use neo-institutional theory along with detailed ethnographic data to reveal how institutional practices come to be legitimated. I did answer these questions, eventually. And, the answer is in this book. I did find e-commerce entrepreneur companies that passionately led fashion companies to the digital age; and, I traveled extensively and interviewed widely fashion companies, whose executives expressed *their own* passionate beliefs as to whether the paradigm of brick-and-mortar was changing, or forever remaining an archetype one couldn't circumvent.

I am grateful to my ethnography 'hosts' at Digital Moda—one of the largest e-commerce fashion companies worldwide—who selflessly permitted me to carry on my observations and interviews both in New York and Milan. Their willingness to answer any questions I came up with, as well as their knowledge, passion, and humility about the fashion industry, will forever mean a lot to this author.

I am also thankful to my colleagues at the remarkable Center for Organizational Innovation (COI) at Columbia University, and especially to my advisor, David Stark. Special thanks also goes to people who provided meaningful advice along the way: Eva Boxenbaum, Micki Eisenman, Priscilla Ferguson, Candace Jones, Gayle Kaufman, Bruce Kogut, Massimo Maoret, and Pilar Opazo-Breton.

Finally, I would be amiss not to mention my gratitude to Keith, who kept the household together while I was frequently away with my thoughts, in another dimension, writing; to John, who spent tireless hours on the phone; and, to "Brian"—one of the greatest, most humble e-commerce innovators there is.

Enjoy the ride!

Sarasota, USA   Iva Petkova

CONTENTS

LIST OF FIGURES

LIST OF TABLES

Introduction: Field Transformations and Institutional Entrepreneurship in Cultural Industries

> We started out as an incubator of ideas for the transitioning of the culture of fashion companies online. We provide them with a set of tools that allow them to be independent. But, they are not experts in E-Commerce and we devise together a strategy for the online world.
>
> —CEO, *Digital Moda*, NYC, 2012

On a crisp winter morning in January of 2012, a lively discussion took place at the New York regional headquarters of *Digital Moda*—an e-commerce fashion company.[1] In the conference room before me the North American CEO, the Head of Merchandising, the Director of Marketing and the Chief Branding Officer discussed how to best approach collaboration with one of the world's largest publishers of monthly fashion media. The talk revolved around a partnership proposed by the conglomerate and its likely effect on the partners of *Digital Moda*—established luxury fashion companies. Skeptically evaluating the online selection of fashion content on one of the largest fashion magazines owned by the publisher, the Head of Merchandising at *Digital Moda* frowned, "curating content to the max, such as presenting merchandise from brands that happen to be this or that blogger's favorite, is unlikely to drive recognition or revenue for us, unless the shopping site that is supposed to sell this curated content also happens to be the site of a well-known brand". The North American CEO sighed, and noted that "the media industry has started to realize that it is productive to link product and content. But, what we want is in any collaboration

I. Petkova, *Engineering Legitimacy*,
https://doi.org/10.1007/978-3-319-90707-9_1

1

for customers to be led to [*our*] content. All this interaction needs to occur online." The Director of Marketing had assessed how the publishing conglomerate approached collaboration with other e-commerce fashion companies and was not impressed. "In their initial proposal, thoughts and progression-wise, they were far beyond others," he noted. "Structurally, however, they still act as paper media publishers. As much as this old player wants to view [*Digital Moda*] as a partner, they are also trying to indeed impress us with their *digital* knowledge". The Chief Branding Officer—a longtime fashion industry editor—settled the discussion. She noted that the online selection of fashion brands featured on the largest in the conglomerate's portfolio of fashion magazines was "… so overcurated. We don't want to niche-fy all of our brands into one property. This is my biggest concern". The CEO completed the collective thought process of the small group: "Publishing firms think: how much can we charge for content, instead of what content should we feature? They will never change, however they progress, unless [*Digital Moda*] tells them how it works".

The above discussion at *Digital Moda* is a fascinating snippet of data illustrating the struggles for legitimacy by online fashion organizations (e-commerce and social commerce) in the institutional field of fashion over the past decade. e-commerce fashion companies, like *Digital Moda*, ShopBop.com, and Asos.com, are retail technology organizations that own and develop electronic commerce and marketing technologies to support their operations. E-commerce fashion companies acquire, promote, and sell branded fashion apparel through an electronic medium and without maintaining retail stores to display their merchandise. Social commerce companies, such as Polyvore.com and ShopStyle.com, are the main partners of e-commerce fashion entrepreneurs. These companies engage in a form of e-commerce that links consumers with curated fashion product, displayed in dedicated online galleries where consumers compete with each other to create looks, and "click-to-buy" fashion product (Khosrow-Pour 2018). E-commerce and social commerce fashion companies are involved in collaboration that combines two ubiquitous institutional advantages in the fashion industry—the aesthetic and the commercial—enjoyed previously only by brick-and-mortar s in the industry, such as Neiman Marcus, and fashion magazines, like Vogue.

Since 2006, *Digital Moda* has operated the e-commerce design, operations, and aspects of digital communications and marketing, for over two-dozen global luxury fashion companies, turning into more than three-dozen brands and growing in 2017. Started by people with no insider knowledge of the fashion industry and driven by the entrepreneurial action of *"simply the doing of new things*, or the doing of things that are already being done in a new way (innovation)" (Schumpeter 1947, p. 151, emphasis added). *Digital Moda* and other e-commerce fashion companies have become accepted as institutional partners by luxury fashion companies, exposing, in the process, traditional fashion companies and their fashion product to a wider global audience, lower price points, and new economic and aesthetic practices. The founders of these new companies frequently referred to their businesses as a *new generation* fashion companies. Their executives typically arrived from financial and investment banking backgrounds and frequently reported to have been culturally influenced by early digital pioneers, like Amazon and eBay. During their fledgling developmental phase, in the beginning of the aughts, these Internet entrepreneurs used e-commerce technology to start their technology-driven fashion businesses, grappling with competing ideas of validating themselves as brand destinations and marketing channels without any direct access to fashion organizations, fashion media publications, or fashion retailers. For the first time in the history of fashion as a creative culture industry, e-commerce and social commerce entrepreneurs—companies with limited formal practice in any of the areas of deep institutional expertise of fashion companies—merchandising, communications, or retailing—and no prior existing ties in the industry, have gained responsibility for operating the e-commerce of established luxury fashion companies, including marketing, and advertising of their branded apparel product.

The case of these new entrepreneurial organizations is a distinctive study that addresses one of the least understood aspects of institutional legitimation in creative culture industries: the mechanisms by which new organizations achieve legitimacy and garner influence in deeply institutionalized culture industry contexts, where incumbent organizations maintain significant gaps between their strategy formulation (i.e., "thinking") and their behavior (i.e., "doing") and exhibit low aspirations for learning (Meyer and Rowan 1977; March 1991). What are the means by which new creator organizations achieve legitimacy and influence over such culture industry behemoths, as fashion companies? Finally, how have long-standing creatures of ritual in culture contexts, like fashion companies, resolved artistic versus commercial conflict that represents for these mature organizations a chief hurdle to accepting new paradigms in their organizational practice?

In laying out the latter inquiry, I should briefly acknowledge that the conclusions of earlier comparative studies in innovation by Christensen (1997), Tushman and O'Reilly (1996) and Christensen and Raynor (2003) still stand. Incumbents across established industries can suffer from dissociative behavior and can exhibit slowness to change in the context of maladaptive practice. Existing players in an industry indelibly fail to appreciate how novelty will affect them, due to the different institutional and business logics operating in these organizations. Newcomer entrepreneurs are, therefore, enabled at least in part, to take advantage of the disruption by creating a viable niche, where they could test new practice that eventually becomes requisite for existing players in a given field. However, creative culture industries present a more complicated reality of adaptation to change than manufacturing contexts do.

This is because fields of cultural production are first, located at an intermediary position "between the artistic field and the economic field" (Bourdieu and Delsaut 1975, p. 22). Second, the classic boundary maintenance between art and commerce across culture industries is but a metaphoric representation of organizational reality in these contexts, as the formal structure of organizations in these domains tends to be loosely related to their actual work repertoires, yet closely related to artistic rhetoric and ritual (Meyer and Rowan 1977; Powell 2012). Finally, against this institutional backdrop, cultural fields are increasingly exposed to interrelated processes of erosion of their external boundaries and to ongoing "transformation of [their] internal hierarchies" (Pedroni and Volonte 2014, p. 102; Crane 2012; Entwistle and Slater 2014). The current evidence for a dynamic transformation occurring in cultural industries can be, in part, attributed to the erosion of the institutional advantage of 'art' in these contexts (*de*-artification); a situation that in some settings field-level constituents attempt to accordingly fortify (*re*-artification) (Shapiro and Heinich 2012). Artification occurs when cultural industries face changes in opportunity spaces, institutionalization, and legitimating ideology that render the existing boundaries between commercial and aesthetic intent untenable. The ambiguity resulting from these ongoing processes of transformation is potentially detrimental to incumbents because constituent organizational actors in these creative culture contexts—executives at various organizational levels, for one—are averse to challenging the upheld validity of aesthetic over commercial intent, and their practice has characteristically supported a striving to become an art form.

Unquestionably, some of these transformational processes have opened up creative contexts to new distribution and marketing channels, such as the digital channel, and through the subsequent emergence of new organizational forms along their boundaries, shifts in power have occurred within their formal structures. In the music industry, for example, organizational transformations are frequently heralded as a radical new development, in which virtual communities of artists and consumers engage in the building of "dynamic and self-organizing entities based on patterns of electronic information interchange" (Hughes and Lang 2003, p. 180). In this respect, particularly in the Scandinavian music industry, the digitization of music contours the emergence of a new "art-entrepreneurship" hypothesis, where relatively new practices, such as self-publishing of music content have become a "trans-disciplinary, multifaceted" (Aggestam 2007, p. 31) paradigm in the making that unites both commercial and aesthetic logic. In other cultural contexts, such as photography, the trend has been to reframe the praxis in this industry from a "middle-brow art" (Bourdieu and Whiteside 1996), concerned more with striving towards the aesthetic and less with developing social practice, to a paradigmatic new method of collective participation and creative expression used in our habitus (Koskinen 2017). Finally, with the emergence of new digital streaming media and video-on-demand online players, like Netflix, there has been a transformational shift in culture contexts producing cultural products that conventionally "could not be defined as 'art'", such as TV drama (Lavie 2015, p. 20). Amazon, Facebook, Google, Match.com, Microsoft, Netflix, Twitter, and other technology-driven companies have altogether transformed the meaning of aesthetics *and* culture, from one connected to the opinion of professional taste-makers, such as TV and film critics, to one in which culture is "algorithmic"; it is understood as an "emergent framework of identification" in which consumers co-participate in the production of aesthetics and taste with the help of algorithms (Hallinan and Striphas 2016, p. 118).

The field of fashion is not impervious to these larger developments. Fashion companies have long maintained organizational siloes that appreciate an institutional separation between art and commerce. On the one hand, fashion companies and their apparel product have been deemed to represent an aesthetic economy (Entwistle and Rocamora

2006; Crane 2012) with no commercial considerations (a practice that Bourdieu and Delsaut in 1975 (p. 28) called "transubstantiation"). Increasingly, however, the fashion industry is depicted as a highly globalized field of commerce that bridges "multiple networks that connect an upstream of suppliers to a downstream of customers through a market interface made of producers" (Aspers and Godart 2013, p. 181). This shift in scholarly interest has importantly revealed that personnel working *outside* the area of design in fashion firms, such as visual merchandisers, have a growing strategic, technical, and procedural influence, even though they engage in producing "forms of creativity that are *different* from designers and communicators" (Mora 2006, p. 349, emphasis added). Milanese designers themselves have embarked on a path of emphasizing a *de*-artified "culture of wearability" in their practice, materialized through the service relation of apparel, rather than in the production of apparel as art (Pedroni and Volonte 2014, p. 110). Communications divisions in fashion firms are, correspondingly, adapting to new modes of cultural production of content, such as blogging, in which they frequently discover the opposing and autonomous messages of fashion bloggers (Pedroni 2015; Rocamora 2013). Finally, as the structure of the high-fashion field changes and its commercial aspects become more apparent, fashion journalists have (as in prior times during the history of the field) become fixated on reconstructing designer fashion as an artistic (*re*-artified) practice (Van de Peer 2014).

Accepting the legitimacy of technology-driven e-commerce fashion organizations and their practice is a significant challenge not only for established fashion companies, but also for essential field constituents, which direct the path of the field—retail consultancies, fashion media, brick-and-mortar retailers, and flagship industry associations (e.g., *British Fashion Council* in the UK, *Fondazione Altagamma* in Italy, CFDA—*Council of Fashion Designers of America* in the United States). The technical knowledge and skills developed by e-commerce and social commerce entrepreneurs could not and did not automatically result in the production of legitimacy vis-à-vis fashion companies. The lack of *prior* cultural support by fashion companies had, in fact, exposed earlier entrants in e-commerce fashion in the 1990s to Stinchcombe's "liability of newness" (1965, p. 148) hypothesis and doomed them to a higher risk of failure (see, e.g., DiMaggio 1988; Zuckerman 1999). In the first ten years of the new century, only a few luxury fashion firms had e-commerce businesses, organizational units that regulated e-commerce, or advertised their brands online. One well-known marketing consultant at a global retail consultancy called this behavior "a response out of apprehension and fear". Another industry pundit interpreted it as a cultural "tantrum" indicating lack of preparedness, awareness, and risk-taking in fashion firms. In short, the well-oiled "cognitive, moral and regulative" (Lounsbury 2008, p. 349) institutional logics operating in fashion companies have converged to problematize the relationship of fashion companies with outsiders (e.g., e-commerce companies), delay the formulation of new commercial goals by fashion executives, and deepen aversion to technology (Crane 1997, 2012; Parkins 2013).

The practices traditionally awarded legitimacy in fashion are linked to creative design, communications, and organizational support of the highly regularized relationship between fashion companies, brick-and-mortar retailers and fashion magazines (Bourdieu 1993a; Godart 2012). My empirical investigation into the work of professionals with strategic and positional influence in areas other than design across five luxury fashion companies in this book demonstrates the existence of two distinct trajectories of adaptation. The first trajectory reveals that fashion company executives can continually choose to convey their support for existing siloes and downplay the introduction of new work practices, even when their executive teams have objectively decided to create e-commerce units within the formal structure. This form of adaptation occurred when established organizational units in some fashion companies, such as Communications or Retail, subsumed e-commerce under their provenance to safeguard the boundary between formal structure and actual work repertoires. Once the unfamiliar practice of e-commerce was placed in an established, well-known organizational silo, it was *re*-artified. An already existing, institutionally legitimated, ceremonial practice was picked to take over e-commerce without concern for the development of actual work repertoires, associated with the new practice. In the second instance, when new executives were hired to define and represent e-commerce in the formal organizational structure, they quickly moved to solidify the new practice and align e-commerce rhetoric with the content of actual work by engaging in a symbolic rebellion for independence—a "resistance against artification" (Shapiro and Heinich 2012)—to support the work of the new unit.

This mentality of active opposition to new organizational practices in fashion companies is hardly beneficial for outsider legitimation and is a product of their low aspirations for learning, yet high sensitivity of complying with the constraints of the institutional environment. Deep investigative accounts have been scarce on detailing the mechanisms used by new organizational dwellers in established institutional fields in culture industries to gain legitimacy. Scholars have, in particular, tended to squarely place *online* businesses as dichotomous conduits of information to larger publics or other businesses. Earlier studies on technology innovation have suggested that online businesses are successful due to their ability to develop a "continually morphing" menu of capabilities (Rindova and Kotha 2001; Hagel 2002). Taxonomy of online organizational forms has also been suggested, based on the capability of online organizations to transmit ever more complex information to consumers or other related firms (Sawhney et al. 2003). In this taxonomy, online companies were relegated to mediating information (thus, the name "infomediaries") or mediating innovation (thus, the title "innomediaries"). Yet, e-commerce and social commerce companies, like *Digital Moda*, have transmitted more than "information" to established fashion companies over time. In fact, these organizations have influenced the development of innovative practices with significant legitimacy to fashion incumbents and the emergence of new behavior in fashion companies, such as the opening up of e-commerce units as part of latter' organizational structures.

In short, cultural intermediaries in the classic Bourdeausian sense, these companies were not. E-commerce and social commerce organizations did not engage in constructing a digital space "authentic" to the existing elites in the fashion field and aspirational to the masses, that the elites were going to abandon once the "masses" had reached it, thus giving rise to cycles of new fashions, and indeed a whole new industry of cultural intermediaries in charge of keeping the high-intensity pace. To the contrary, by developing a collectively legitimated template of common cultural values in which their legitimizing rhetoric was aligned with the egalitarian ideology of their own base of operations—the Internet—new organizations in digital fashion developed a fundamental 'logic of confidence' vis-à-vis the brick-and-mortar fashion field 'proper' (Meyer and Rowan 1977; see, also, Suddaby and Greenwood 2005). Their executives dictated rules in that space, crosscutting the technical environment of these entrepreneurial technology players and looking to legitimize their innovative practice in the institutionally elaborated field of fashion.

E-commerce and social commerce organizations frequently educated each other on the value of their new practices. Before the role of adopters was conferred to fashion companies, it was initially played by other peers in the community, who shared templates of behavior and rhetoric, and partook in ceremonies of mutual affirmation (typically, fast-paced start-up celebration events in New York City), while educating and facilitating the access of other members to new technology (Shah and Tripsas 2007; Garud and Karnøe 2003). Within their own community, e-commerce and social commerce companies were incentivized to collaborate, in order to better control the ambiguity of their own technical environment. In the absence of digital fashion institutions that governed their behavior, and of professional level audiences that sanctioned their work, orientation with regard to each other's work priorities, and the advantage of receiving feedback through their own community did the job (White 2002; Tripsas 2009). This situation created advantages for both types of organization, insofar as it allowed each to establish dominant position in interpreting the uses of e-commerce and social commerce technology to insiders in their self-defined group in digital fashion.

My remedy to this fundamental puzzle of outsider legitimation in cultural fields was ultimately resolved by Woody Powell's recent invitation to use neo-institutional theory along with "detailed ethnographic studies that reveal how institutional practices come to be legitimated" (2012, p. 201). In the case of the fashion industry, an ethnographic study had to scrutinize multiple layers of legitimacy that e-commerce entrepreneurs might encounter. In 1995, Mark Suchman developed two perspectives—strategic and institutional—in gauging the prospects for gains in legitimacy by new organizations. These perspectives required that two types of legitimacy—moral and pragmatic—were sought by new organizations. The institutional perspective maintained that new entrepreneurs need to gain cultural support for their actions based on the *moral* approval of established players; in this case, fashion companies and field-level professional fashion organizations (cf. Meyer and Scott 1983). The strategic view offered that new organizations should strive to gain *pragmatic* legitimacy by involving themselves into a direct economic exchange with established constituencies. Suchman (1995, p. 574) had also provided one of the finest (and broadest) definitions of legitimacy around—as "a generalized perception or assumption that the actions of an entity are desirable, proper or appropriate within some socially constructed system of norms, values, beliefs and definitions".

In the case of e-commerce and social commerce entrepreneurs, I considered that both moral and pragmatic legitimacy should be investigated. The reason was that although the technical environment of e-commerce and social commerce companies required them to "'get the job done'" (Suchman 1995, p. 603), in this case, by developing efficient practices in e-commerce—and, obviously, attempting to be commercially successful—the institutional environment of fashion companies would require these new organizations to "'make sense'" (ibid., p. 604; see also, Deephouse and Suchman 2008) to established players. Moral legitimacy was the harder thing to establish. Whereas pragmatic legitimacy was established by the development of an "acceptable commercial practice" (Scardaville 2009, p. 366), moral legitimacy was a wholly distinctive object of analysis.

The following historical example illustrates the importance of moral legitimacy, or lack thereof, for a pioneering e-commerce fashion retailer—Bluefly, Inc.—founded in 1998. Despite creating an authoritative voice in its first filing with the Securities and Exchange Commission (SEC) on the intent to develop "eight future principal elements of success" (Bluefly Inc. 2001, p. 6) for the hopeful field of e-commerce fashion, Bluefly was unable to gain cultural acceptance by fashion companies. Even though company executives continued to highlight over the years their projected goal of acquiring premium matrix of fashion brands for Bluefly's e-commerce website, as early as 2002 the management team conceded to purchasing fashion apparel both directly from fashion brand owners and *indirectly* from third-party distributors. Furthermore, the company apparently intended to expand relationships with "suppliers of end-of-season and excess name brand apparel and fashion accessories" (Bluefly Inc. 2002, p. 25). Industry pundits and fashion company executives reinforced these historical arguments. A merchandising executive in one luxury fashion company expressed disapproval impatiently in an interview in 2011: "No, no. It's an online outlet: opposite mentality! Price and order delivery is important, but it's opposite *mentality!*" The Director of a flagship European fashion association noted that "Bluefly was an experiment; online outlet. Buying leftovers; very well done, but very simple". In April 2012, after fourteen years in the business of e-commerce, Bluefly reported accumulated financial deficit of over $162,485,000 (Bluefly Inc. 2012). As Bluefly's example suggests, accomplishing both categories of legitimacy can be a protracted social process that is easily compared to the four-stage process of diffusion of innovations consisting of innovation, local validation, diffusion, and general validation (Johnson et al. 2006).

The power of the institutional view is evident here in explaining how to study moral legitimacy. New organizations will seek *"cultural support"*—and therefore, moral legitimacy—of a very specific nature. Their own rationale for existence will have to align with "established cultural accounts [...] for its existence, functioning, and jurisdiction" (Meyer and Scott 1983, p. 201) at the level of incumbent organizations in the fashion field. The fact that these accounts have to be *established* (as well as *"credible [and] collective"* (Suchman 1995, p. 575, emphasis added) put e-commerce and social commerce organizations at a greater risk. Their materialization as outsiders in the fashion industry at the dawn of the 2000s compounded the unlikelihood that these entrepreneurial ventures will have accumulated credible collection of accounts from field organizations in the fashion industry, or that they would have been perceived as legitimate in the field. The hypothesis that there needed to be *general* validation, in particular, also suggested that once e-commerce companies had acquired credibility in the eyes of fashion constituents, they thenceforth had to actively mobilize these moral commitments and transform them into accepted commercial practice. The goal was, apparently, to continue being evaluated positively by fashion companies and their constituents (Suchman 1995).

I discovered that e-commerce and social commerce companies engage in a three-stage mechanism for gaining legitimacy, which ensures that their moral desirability is combined with pragmatic influence. When faced with challenges resulting from a lack of moral legitimacy, e-commerce and social commerce companies initiated the development of *narratives for legitimization* in the field. Curiously, these narratives markedly diverged from those of established field-level organizations and persisted without active support from fashion elites in the field. Within their own community, e-commerce entrepreneurs employed narratives for legitimization as rhetorical devices that are "oriented to collectively defined, and often collectively mandated, ends" (Meyer and Rowan 1977, p. 349). Narratives for legitimization really characterized the "digital" entry point for e-commerce fashion entrepreneurs in the field. Their role was twofold. By creating narratives for legitimization their existence, e-commerce entrepreneurs engineered an acceptable account of shared "cultural logics" (Rao and Giorgi 2006) that were critical to the successful functioning of the new e-commerce field. The work on validating these accounts was among the most important facets of performance for new entrepreneurs, because, ultimately, shared logics had to be successfully communicated to fashion companies at the threshold of "making sense" (Suchman 1995, p. 575) for incumbents.

The second component of gaining legitimacy included *actions* on the part of e-commerce and social commerce companies to further formalize their accounts of legitimacy—now established— into an acceptable commercial practice. Using Suchman's (1995) distinction, e-commerce fashion entrepreneurs, essentially, transitioned from the moral legitimacy of "making sense" to the pragmatic legitimacy of "having value" in the fashion field. This was not the end of the road, however, since pragmatic legitimacy needs to be sustained by extending it to a more specific form of legitimacy, to which I refer as *influence* legitimacy. The production of this latter form of legitimacy revealed an interesting tactic on the part of e-commerce fashion entrepreneurs that was eerily similar to lobbying tactics social movements had used in facilitating their own organizational expansion (cf. Bromley et al. 1999). For companies in digital fashion the expansion of influence was achieved by developing explicit tactics that handed over some aspect of the partnership to fashion companies. One such exceptional tactic was the '*culture premium*', about to be explained in the following chapters, that allowed e-commerce and social commerce companies to influence the future direction in which established fashion companies would approach new areas of practice that their executives had never encountered before, in online marketing, social media, or advertising.

Ultimately, this book is about an unpredictable adventure with a surprising result. It is about new organizational players, driven by technology and curiosity, lacking credibility, yet acting brashly in a changing, highly institutionalized cultural industry context. This story is also about mature incumbents representing some of the most visible international luxury fashion brands, that handled novelty ripe with apprehension and fear, swerving between *de-* and *re*-artification of their product from and into the category of art, as their executives kept changing positions, navigating the complex path to adaptation to innovation and change. The adventure about to follow, takes us through Milan, Paris, London, and New York on an entrancing high-tech journey of understanding fashion as a changing terrain of aesthetic and commercial culture in the twenty-first century.

NOTE

1. The name is a pseudonym.

BIBLIOGRAPHY

Aggestam, M. (2007). Art-entrepreneurship in the Scandinavian music industry. In *Entrepreneurship in the creative industries: An international perspective*, 30–53. Edward Elgar Publishing.

Andreessen, M. (2011). Why software is eating the world. *Wall Street Journal*, August 20.

Aspers, P., & Godart, F. (2013). Sociology of fashion: Order & change. *Annual Review of Sociology, 39*, 171–192.

Bluefly, Inc. (2001). *Form 10-K* Annual Report *2001*. Available from: SEC EDGAR website http://www.sec.gov/edgar.shtml. [25 May 2017].

Bluefly, Inc. (2002). *Form 10-K* Annual Report *2000*. Available from: SEC EDGAR website http://www.sec.gov/edgar.shtml. [25 May 2017].

Bluefly, Inc. (2012). *Form 10-K* Annual Report *2000*. Available from: SEC EDGAR website http://www.sec.gov/edgar.shtml. [25 May 2017].

Bourdieu, P. (1993a). Haute culture and haute couture. In Bourdieu, P. (Ed.), *Sociology in Question*, 132–138. London: Sage.

Bourdieu, P. (1993b). *The field of cultural production: Essays on art and literature*. Cambridge: Polity.

Bourdieu, P., & Delsaut, Y. (1975). Le couturier et sa griffe: Contribution à une théorie de la magie. *Actes de la Recherche en Sciences Sociales, 1*(1), 7–36.

Bourdieu, P., & Whiteside, S. (1996). *Photography: A middle-brow art*. Stanford: Stanford University Press.

Bromley, D. G., Cutchin, D. G., Gerlach, L. P., Green, J. C., Halcli, A., Hirsch, E. L., Jasper, J. M., Jenkins, J. C., Johnson, R. A., McAdam, D., & Meyer, D. S. (1999). *Waves of protest: Social movements since the sixties*. Rowman & Littlefield Publishers.

Christensen, C. M. (1997). *The innovator's dilemma, when new technologies cause great firms to fail*. Harvard Business Review Press.

Christensen, C. M., & Raynor, M. E. (2003). *The innovator's solution: Creating and sustaining successful growth*. Harvard Business Review Press.

Crane, D. (1997). Globalization, organizational size, and innovation in the French luxury fashion industry: Production of culture theory revisited. *Poetics, 24*(6), 393–414.

Crane, D. (2012). *Fashion and its social agendas: Class, gender, and identity in clothing*. Chicago: University of Chicago Press.

Deephouse, D. L., & Suchman, M. (2008). Legitimacy in organizational institutionalism. *The Sage Handbook of Organizational Institutionalism, 49,* 77.

DiMaggio, P.J. (1988). Interest & agency in institutional theory. *Institutional Patterns & Organizations, Culture & Environment, 1,* 3–22.

Entwistle, J., & Rocamora, A. (2006). The field of fashion materialized: A study of London fashion week. *Sociology, 40*(4), 735–751.

Entwistle, J., & Slater, D. (2014). Reassembling the cultural: Fashion models, brands and the meaning of 'culture' after ANT. *Journal of Cultural Economy, 7*(2), 161–177.

Garud, R., & Karnøe. P. (2003). Bricolage versus breakthrough: Distributed and embedded agency in technology entrepreneurship. *Research Policy, 32*(2), 277–300.

Godart, F. (2012). *Unveiling fashion: Business, culture, & identity in the most glamorous industry.* Springer.

Hagel, J. (2002). Web services and the development of value chains, insights from John Hagel. *Internet World.*

Hallinan, B. & Striphas, T. (2016). Recommended for you: The Netflix Prize and the production of algorithmic culture. *New Media & Society, 18*(1), 117–137.

Hughes, J., & Lang, K.R. (2003). If I had a song: The culture of digital community networks and its impact on the music industry. *International Journal on Media Management, 5*(3), 180–189.

Johnson, C., Dowd, T.J., & Ridgeway, C.L. (2006). Legitimacy as a social process. *Annual Review of Sociology, 32,* 53–78.

Khosrow-Pour, M. (2018). *Encyclopedia of Information Science and Technology,* Fourth.

Koskinen, I., (2017). *Mobile multimedia in action.* Routledge.

Lavie, N. (2015). Israeli drama: constructing the Israeli 'quality' television series as an art form. *Media, Culture & Society, 37*(1), 19–34.

Lounsbury, M. (2008). Institutional rationality & practice variation: New directions in the institutional analysis of practice. *Accounting, Organizations & Society, 33*(4–5), 349–361.

March, J.G. (1991). Exploration and exploitation in organizational learning. *Organization Science, 2*(1), 71–87.

Meyer, J.W., & Rowan, B. (1977). Institutionalized organizations: Formal structure as myth and ceremony. *American Journal of Sociology, 83*(2), 340–363.

Meyer, J.W., & Scott, W.R. (1983). Centralization and the legitimacy problems of local government. In Meyer, J.W., & Scott, W.R. (Eds.) *Organizational environments: Ritual and rationality.* Newbury Park: Sage.

Mora, E. (2006). Collective production of creativity in the Italian fashion system. *Poetics, 34*(6), 334–353.

Parkins, I. (2013). *Poiret, Dior & Schiaparelli: Fashion, femininity & modernity.* London and New York: A&C Black.

Pedroni, M. (2015). "Stumbling on the heels of my blog": Career, forms of capital, and strategies in the (sub)field of fashion blogging. *Fashion Theory, 19*(2), 179–199.

Pedroni, M., & Volonté, P. (2014). Art seen from outside: Non-artistic legitimation within the field of fashion design. *Poetics, 43,* 102–119.

Powell, W.W. (2012). Expanding the scope of institutional analysis. In DiMaggio, P.J., & Powell, W.W. (Eds.), *The new institutionalism in organizational analysis,* 183–201. Chicago, IL: University of Chicago Press.

Rao, H., & Giorgi, S. (2006). Code breaking: How entrepreneurs exploit cultural logics to generate institutional change. *Research in Organization Behavior, 27,* 269–304.

Rocamora, A. (2013). How new are new media? The case of fashion blogs. In Bartlett, D., Cole, S., & Rocamora, A. (Eds.), *Fashion media: Past and present,* 155–164. London and New York: Bloomsbury.

Rindova, V.P., & Kotha, S. (2001). Continuous 'morphing': Competing through dynamic capabilities, form, and function. *Academy of Management Journal, 44*(6), 1263–1280.

Sawhney, M., Prandelli, E., & Verona, G. (2003). The power of Innomediation. *MIT Sloan Management Review, 44*(2), 77–82.

Scardaville, M.C. (2009). High art, no art: The economic & aesthetic legitimacy of US soap operas. *Poetics, 37*(4), 366–382.

Schumpeter, J.A. (1947). The creative response in economic history. *The Journal of Economic History, 7*(02), 149–159.

Shah, S.K., & Tripsas, M. (2007). The accidental entrepreneur: The emergent and collective process of user entrepreneurship. *Strategic Entrepreneurship Journal, 1*(1–2), 123–140.

Shapiro, R., & Heinich, N. (2012). When is artification? *Contemporary Aesthetics, 4*(April 5), 1–12. Retrieved from: http://www.contempaesthetics.org/newvolume/pages/article.php?articleID=639.

Simmel, G. (1957). Fashion. *American Journal of Sociology, 62*(6, May), 541–558.

Stinchcombe, A.L. (1965). Social structure & organizations. In March, J.G. (Ed.), *Handbook of Organizations,* 142–193. Chicago: Rand McNally.

Suchman, M. (1995). Managing legitimacy, strategic & institutional approaches. *Academy of Management Review, 20*(3), 571–610.

Suddaby, R., & Greenwood, R. (2005). Rhetorical strategies of legitimacy. *Administrative Science Quarterly, 50*(1), 35–67.

Tripsas, M. (2009). Technology, identity and inertia, through the lens of 'the digital photography company'. *Organization Science, 20*(2), 441–460.

Tushman, M., & O'Reilly, C. (1996). Evolution and revolution: Mastering the dynamics of innovation and change. *California Management Review, 38*(4), 8–30.

Van de Peer, A. (2014). Re-artification in a world of de-artification: Materiality and intellectualization in fashion media discourse 1949–2010. *Cultural Sociology, 8*(4), 443–461.

White, H.C. (2002). *Markets from networks: Socioeconomic models of production.* Princeton: Princeton University Press.

Zuckerman, E.W., (1999). The categorical imperative: Securities analysts and the illegitimacy discount. *American Journal of Sociology, 104*(5), 1398–1438.

CHAPTER 2

New Institutional Entrepreneurs in the Fashion Industry

So, for me E-Commerce is everything; the buying, the selling, the web marketing and the tech.

CEO, *Digital Moda*, New York City

DEMOGRAPHY AND CULTURE IN AN EMERGING INSTITUTIONAL FIELD[1]

By 2010, the institutional field of fashion had significantly changed. New start-up companies in e-commerce and social commerce were created. Journalistic accounts at the time suggested that these new entrepreneurial ventures were veritable 'gods-of-the-gaps' that emerged to "fill the void left by the big brands" (Walmsley 2008).

As an organizational practice, e-commerce is both an economic and an aesthetic activity. Laudon and Traver (2003, p. 10) have demarcated e-commerce as the "entire world of electronically based organizational activities that support a firm's market exchanges—including a firm's entire information system's infrastructure that enables interactivity between merchants and consumers in planning and delivering communications". E-commerce companies are often referred to as "pure-play" in the e-commerce literature, to distinguish between online retailers and traditional brick-and-mortar merchants. In its December 2006 issue, the popular *Internet Retailer* periodical first defined the term, noting that "[v]isits to pure-play web retailers in Nielsen/NetRatings Inc. Holiday

© The Author(s) 2018
I. Petkova, *Engineering Legitimacy*,
https://doi.org/10.1007/978-3-319-90707-9_2

eShopping index were 54 per cent greater than visits to multi-channel retailers in the index" (Brohan 2006).

E-commerce fashion retailers, like *Digital Moda* and *Luxemod*, were founded as early as 2000. These companies founded their businesses as proprietary technology platforms, acquiring and selling branded fashion apparel. Their knowledge and skills at the early stages were associated with an e-commerce start-up (Table 2.1); a company that specializes in developing proprietary technology infrastructure in electronic business, integrates front-end Web presence and back-end information systems (IS), facilitates transactions, manages inventory, and improves customer services (Zhu 2004, p. 168). E-commerce companies were able to gain cultural support from established fashion companies, securing the ability to acquire fashion merchandise *directly* from fashion companies and display their branded product on their own e-commerce websites. Achieving this moral legitimacy permitted some e-commerce retailers, most notably, *Digital Moda*, to extend their skills in the field, moving from e-commerce retail to e-commerce consulting and digital media and marketing (Table 2.1). By acquiring this skill, *Digital Moda*, in particular, has gained an augmented role in the fashion industry extending to building, running, and maintaining marketing products and e-commerce websites *for* fashion companies.

Table 2.1   E-commerce and social commerce companies—Evolution in practice

Company	Evolution in practice[a]				
	E-commerce start-up	E-commerce consultant	Social commerce collaboration	Co-branding	Creative control over co-branding
Digital Moda	[2000]	[2006]	[2008]	[2010]	[2011/2012]
Luxemod	[2000]	[2012]		[2010]	
Samplemod	[2007]			[2010]	
Boutiquemod	[2010]			[2011]	
Digidesigner	[2010]			[2011]	
Rent-a-Mod	[2010]				
StyleMag			[2006]	[2010]	
CommunityMag			[2009]	[2010]	

[a]Year when the practice was launched

Social commerce companies were launched around 2006 as fashion search platforms combining search and recommendation features with e-commerce fashion retail (see, *StyleMag*, *CommunityMag*—Table 2.1). Known also as 'participatory commerce', 'user-curated shopping' platforms, and "Google for Fashion",[2] social commerce companies redirect consumers to e-commerce fashion retailers that carry the desired item to make the actual purchase. The combination of search technology with e-commerce fashion retailing reflected the assertion of social commerce founders that consumers and "users have a strong inclination to seek information from others during the search process" (Chi 2009, p. 42). The implication was that combining targeted search with advertising campaigns would lead consumers to browse in order to buy.

Social commerce companies can be distilled in two categories— brick-and-mortar magazines that journeyed online by founding digital divisions (Vogue.com, Elle.com, MarieClaire.com, or InStyle.com) and 'pure play' companies, born online. DesignerApparel.com, ShopStyle. com, Polyvore.com, Refinery29.com, Nylon.com and the now-defunct Boutiques.com, previously founded by Google, exemplify the second type.

Culturally, social commerce companies on the Internet have evolved from the simpler functionality of price-comparison engines (PCE). In late 1990s, PCEs were the online 'places' where shoppers went to learn about the options of finding diverse products, as fragrance, flowers, or computers, frequently searching for the lowest price. PCEs crawled the Internet for relevant results, ranking retailers that sold the product in order of pricing. Although the typical source of revenue for social commerce companies remained tied to commission-based agreements with e-commerce fashion retailers, price was no longer the sole selective filter in generating results for prospective customers who browsed. The algorithm designed by social commerce engineers took other variables into consideration, such as *relevance* of the fashion brand, fashion style, seasonal theme, and name of the fashion brand and e-commerce retailer.

EARLY EXPERIMENTS IN THE EMERGING FIELD OF DIGITAL FASHION

To appreciate the difference in institutionalizing intent between later e-commerce and social commerce companies and early experiments of e-commerce pioneers in fashion, this section provides a brief review of two companies, founded in the late 1990s, with the intent of becoming leaders in their respective areas of luxury branded fashion and handbags. Interviewees in e-commerce and social commerce companies had noted that these early models had limited success. The Global Director of Marketing at *Digital Moda* noted that the founders of early e-commerce ventures approached the online channel with the "brusque sensitivity" of brick-and-mortar retailers such as Nordstrom and Saks. In fact, e-commerce and social commerce executives have argued that the earliest e-commerce pioneers, founded in the institutional domain of digital fashion, were "failures in culture". The CEO of *Digital Moda* in the United States asserted that from a "cultural technology perspective, these [companies] are technology spillovers" forked in between an identity mindful of appreciating their online "roots" and, yet, petrified of experimenting with fashion outside of the cultural tenets of the mainstream paradigm.

BLUEFLY.COM

Bluefly.com was founded as one of the first e-commerce fashion companies online and its founding firm, Bluefly Inc. went public in 2000, immediately after the launch of the venture. The intent of Bluefly's founders is evident in the company's 10-K Report in 2001—an annual report required by the US Securities and Exchange Commission (SEC), containing a detailed summary of a company's financial performance. The intent of executive officers was to build a retail brand online, similar to a luxury department store, but with the caveat that it would "*selectively* acquire end-of-season and excess inventory of high-end designer fashion products and create a hybrid retail environment, that combines the best of the 3 traditional channels: full-price department stores, catalogs and traditional off-price stores" (Bluefly, Inc. 2001).

Bluefly's e-commerce platform was built by *Blue Martini*, a small and at the time-independent software firm, with which the company signed a Software License Agreement in March 2002. Bluefly's e-retail team accorded substantial importance to the optimization of their e-commerce operation. The company's 10-K in 2001 asserted that "with the assistance of consultants from Blue Martini, we plan to develop an improved version of our website based on Blue Martini software. Once launched, we expect that the upgraded website will provide us with better tools to create and manage on-site marketing promotions, more robust analytical tools to measure the performance of onsite promotions, greater site stability and a more efficient platform". Bluefly's team aspired to offer customers the advantages of online technology, such as "personalized shopping environment". The website was designed in mind with the customer to "come to Bluefly.com first for all of your fashion needs", and announced the company's ultimate goal: "acquisition of top designer merchandise at a discount and outstanding customer service in a friendly, convenient, upscale environment" (Bluefly, Inc. 2001).

Bluefly was among the first e-commerce companies in fashion to engage in a legitimacy quest with fashion companies. The company founders indicated that it was possible to create practices that would serve as a roadmap for future e-commerce businesses in online fashion. In its first SEC filing in 1998, after the 'hard' launch of www.bluefly.com, the company's C-level management spelled out "eight future principal elements of success"—or, elements of practice—considered noteworthy to establishing institutional competency in the emerging field of digital fashion. Four of these were linked to traditional practices developed by larger brick-and-mortar fashion retailers, like Neiman Marcus or Saks. These elements were price, convenience, customer service, order delivery performance and merchandise selection. The other three elements, "brand recognition", "website performance", and "content" were specific to doing business online. Content was particularly important for success. Bluefly's team gauged that the success of "content" as a signature element would be determined by the popularity of fashion brands acquired and presented on its e-commerce website.

In the years between 1997 and 2000, Bluefly's e-commerce strategy faced the challenge of a cultural disconnect between the stated goals and actual practice. In the absence of advanced e-commerce, social media, and social commerce technologies during that period, the institutional field of digital fashion was a perfunctory channel for fashion brands that had ambiguous meaning to both insider e-commerce players and outside fashion companies, and served an unidentified consumer. Bluefly noted these problems of interpretation of its domain in two consecutive 10-K reports in 2001 and 2002, stating that "[T]he Internet is a rapidly changing and highly competitive market and we *may not have adequate resources to compete successfully.* [...] It is characterized by (a) rapid technological change; (b) evolving user requirements; (c) frequent new product, service and technology introductions; (d) the emergence of new industry practices" (Bluefly, Inc. 2001, 2002).

The fledgling e-commerce company continued interpreting its position in the emerging new channel and spend resources on understanding how it may differ in terms of practice with regard to other existing and incoming players. In 2001 and 2002, Bluefly's executive team enumerated the categories of players most likely to play competition with the company. One category consisted of established and existing land-based retailers, such as Neiman Marcus, Saks, The Gap, Nordstrom, and Macy's. In the other group were traditional direct marketers such as J. Crew, TV marketers, and land-based off-price retail stores. The fact that Bluefly's management positioned the company as directly competing with brick-and-mortar fashion companies signified the ambiguity that they experienced with regard to its structural position in the emerging entrepreneurial field of digital fashion. The relative absence of online e-commerce competitors made brick-and-mortar competitors among the few viable known companies in the field of fashion, with unknown future intentions. Bluefly's management consistently grappled with the question if these brick-and-mortar retailers "[…] may or may not use the Internet in the future to grow their customer base".

Bluefly's executive team likewise charted another emerging category in the new digital space of "less established companies", like Ashford and eLuxury (Bluefly, Inc. 2001, 2002). The company's team conceptualized the two categories of competitors as dissimilar. Brick-and-mortars deciding to open up e-commerce divisions were thought to "use the Internet to expand their channels of distribution". Emerging e-commerce fashion companies, as Ashford and eLuxury were considered to be "building their brands online". Bluefly's team also expected many "additional competitors to emerge in the future".

The management team at Bluefly's was resolute to see the Internet as a quintessential commercial platform for their business. In 2010, Bluefly's annual SEC report specified that the company, in fact, could *not* become the "Store of First Resort for Fashion" *without* using Internet as a distribution and marketing platform. Bluefly interpreted its own identity as a radical e-commerce game changer. At the same time, the e-commerce company identified two additional elements of institutional success for other emerging e-commerce companies on the Internet. The first element was to provide "consistency" in the selection of fashion brands by acquiring a premium matrix of branded fashion product. The second element was to offer online distribution to fashion brands with "scarce" distribution channels.

Notwithstanding these rhetorical objectives, fashion companies remained disinclined to collaborating with Bluefly and averse to the 8 stated elements of practice developed by Bluefly's executive team. In December 2011, after fourteen years of experimenting with e-commerce, Bluefly reported accumulated financial deficit of over $147,468,000. The management team attributed the negative growth to "costs associated with *developing* and *marketing* our Web site and building our infrastructure" (Bluefly, Inc. 2011, emphasis added). In retrospect, challenges with technology and practice were frequently attributed as the two factors that resulted in the acquisition of Bluefly by the Los Angeles private equity firm Clearlake Capital Group LP for $13 million.

Bluefly's executive team started out with good intentions. In the company's two first annual SEC statements, in 2001 and 2002, Bluefly reported that the merchandising strategy of the firm is to enter into *direct* purchasing agreements with fashion designers and fashion brands. The executive team asserted that their buyers have substantial merchandising knowledge gained from former tenures with large fashion retailers, such as Saks, Bergdorf, and Henri Bendel. Despite this claim, Bluefly's team conceded as early as 2001 to purchasing "merchandise both directly from brand owners and indirectly from retailers and third-party distributors" (Bluefly, Inc. 2001). The company was forced to disclose the intent to expand relationships with "suppliers of end-of-season and excess name brand apparel and fashion accessories" and, in addition, to "[…] acquire certain goods on consignment, or leasing or partnering with strategic partners and distributors" (Bluefly, Inc. 2002). Bluefly's executives also acknowledged that merchandise from third parties "increases the risk that we will mistakenly purchase and sell non-authentic or damaged goods" (Bluefly, Inc. 2002).

The other area of concern was the lack of proprietary e-commerce technology for building and maintaining signature elements of practice for Bluefly's growing brand. The cases in this book will demonstrate that internal development of e-commerce would have allowed Bluefly to make its own institutional footprint in practice, instead of heavy dependence on third parties in this area of practice. The first two 10-K annual reports revealed how critical technology was in building the desired "brand recognition" online. Any perceived inconsistencies in Bluefly's e-commerce platform were a "material adverse impact on our business, prospects, financial condition and results of operations" (Bluefly, Inc. 2002). The 10-K reports of 2001 and 2002 also advised shareholders that "[T]here is no assurance that our technology systems will be able to handle increased traffic. Transaction processing systems, network infrastructure, need to be expanded and upgraded; otherwise [this] could 'adversely affect consumers' perceptions of our *brand name*'" (Bluefly, Inc. 2002).

Even though Bluefly's venture in the emerging institutional field of digital fashion remained largely ill-fated, two of the factors that the company team had developed to ensure interest from established fashion brands—content and the ownership of e-commerce technology—became key measures for gaining legitimacy by e-commerce and social commerce companies. The Chief Information Officer (CIO) at *MilanModa1*—one of the key figures at a high-fashion Milanese company featured in this book—understood the critical importance of positive response from fashion companies: "No, no. It's not like our mentality!" he countered impatiently, "It's an online outlet; opposite *mentality!*" A global fashion consultant in a series of discussions underscored that "Bluefly was an *experiment*; online outlet. Buying leftovers from fashion firms, very well done but very simple. They never made a dime".

eLUXURY.COM

eLuxury.com employed a distinct experimental flavor among e-commerce pioneers in digital fashion. The company was launched in 2000 by the luxury fashion conglomerate LVMH Moët Hennessy/Louis Vuitton S.A. Similar to Bluefly, eLuxury planned to become a premier online destination for buying luxury handbags. The company represented one of the rare instances of ideal-typical e-commerce player in an emerging institutional field, because it wielded the direct support of LVMH in distributing their product. Despite this vantage point, on Friday, June 26, 2009, eLuxury.com shut down its e-commerce. The mass email to the list of subscribers stated that the company was "now moving to the next step of its evolution repositioning itself as a premier source of editorial content, information, and inspiration for luxury customers around the world". The open community email stated that eLuxury remained a "[…] pioneer in luxury e-commerce and served as the launching pad for many of the world's most famous luxury brands" (PRWeb 2009). The result was a seeming paradox. Despite the financial backing of LVMH, during its long-term tenure online between 2000 and 2009, eLuxury generated a little over $80 million per year in sales, trailing trailed more than 50% behind the annual sales of Neiman Marcus' online arm, www. neimanmarcus.com.

Global fashion consultants asserted that the conclusion of eLuxury was pointing to a lack of *differentiation* on *product* offered on its e-commerce front. The CEO of the New York-based Luxury Institute, LLC reflected in May 2010 that, "there are dozens of luxury handbags and yes, there is hierarchy, but when we see the results of our surveys, few stand out, like Hermes and Chanel, and then there are 40 that are ranked almost identically by wealthy consumers". In short, the lack of curation of fashion product representing other segments of the handbag market was detrimental to achieving institutional legitimacy in the digital field of fashion. Other luxury industry experts noted that when brick-and-mortar fashion companies, such as LVMH entered e-commerce, the traditional assumption among their executives was to establish the value of their brands on the Internet by replicating their commercial and marketing value proposition of doing business 'offline'.

Digital Moda's Chief Commercial Officer (CCO) reasoned that eLuxury's closure was precipitated by the parent company's lack of "ability to *notice the opportunities*" that existed at the time in carving niche for its existing brand and product online. Just as Bluefly perceived its signature proposition to be alignment with the commercial and marketing approach of powerful brick-and-mortar retailers (Neiman Marcus; Saks), so did eLuxury's executives conceive that e-commerce was an extension—online equivalent—of its controlling parent company, LVMH. The Chief Executive Officer at one of the largest retailers in the fashion industry supported the idea that brick-and-mortar players should differentiate their commercial and marketing approach online from the brick-and-mortar logic of "chasing after the same clients". "One of the important things we have to think about is", she said:

> *What's happening to our brand with all these changes?* Where are the customers going; what is next in terms of change; and finally, where are we going to place our bets? We are a fashion retailer, and we buy merchandise, and year-by-year and season-by-season, we have to think about where we will be placing our bets on merchandise, and where we would be placing our merchandise, once the season is over.

After running deeply discounted prices on premier fashion product during the last weeks of its e-commerce operation, on Tuesday, December 15, 2009, eLuxury became an online magazine, NOWNESS.com. In this iteration, NOWNESS specializes in the curation of content across the cultural domains of "art, design, fashion, beauty, music, food, and travel" (NOWNESS 2017). The transformation of eLuxury.com to Nowness.com stripped the site of its original e-commerce orientation and reoriented the space away from its former explicit association with LVMH and into the domain of content production, curation, and hosting across cultural industries.

THE TRANSFORMATION OF NARRATIVES FOR LEGITIMIZATION INTO MORAL LEGITIMACY

The analysis of the discourses and practice of e-commerce companies in Table 2.1 revealed the existence of *narratives for legitimization* that demonstrate how their founders (frequently, serving as CEOs) aligned their actual knowledge and skill in e-commerce with their projected identity as legitimate partners for fashion companies. The accounts of e-commerce companies entwine and overlap, but rarely conflict with each other. Lacking formal relationships with fashion companies, the founders of e-commerce fashion companies, in particular, grappled with producing organizational stories that sought to "legitimise (and indeed intellectualise) their own areas of expertise" (Cronin 2004, p. 351).

E-commerce and social commerce fashion companies mobilized their legitimation work without active support from established elites in the field. An example of absence of cultural support is the negation of their cultural value by professional fashion organizations during the worst years of the financial crisis, between 2008 and 2010. The Vice President of a global retail management firm, headquartered in NYC, argued in late 2009 that e-commerce fashion companies founded at the outset of the financial crisis (e.g., *Samplemod, Boutiquemod*, and *Digidesigner*) should not be supported by the fashion industry, precisely because of their lack of moral legitimacy:

> Those supply-chains *only* exist because brands made a mistake, ok? As a whole, they're not really viable, but more importantly, they're not solid. [...] I do not even look at those as supply-chains, even though they technically are.

Another senior retail management executive at a retail consulting company shared similar thoughts and argued that both e-commerce and social commerce companies were "opportunistic":

> There's no consistency in what to study. They would be doing whatever's available to them. [...] I think that a smaller company aggregating luxury goods has popped up a lot during many years, but the real players that are able to survive are the likes of Saks and Neiman Marcus.

Alignment with the values of fashion companies was complicated by the fact that e-commerce and social commerce companies were representative of technical environments, in which organizations "are rewarded for effective and efficient control of the work process" (Meyer and Scott 1983, p. 140), instead of reaping rewards for their degree of embeddedness with field-level organizations (DiMaggio and Powell 1983; Powell 2012a, b). The CEO of *Digital Moda*, for example, according to the Chief Technology Evangelist (CTE) based in New York, was a consultant who "is fond of technology as a user. He was *outside of the fashion world*". The organizational identity of *Digital Moda* was initiated, as per the CCO, by "20 people in a basement with very limited connection to the fashion system and with an idea". This identity is intensely similar to the stories of Internet pioneers in e-commerce and Social Media, whose founders started in "garages" (Amazon, Google), "dorm rooms" (Facebook), and "living rooms" (eBay) before eventually becoming household brand names.

Since most pure play founders started out as technology entrepreneurs, the proposition of their teams to carry merchandise from high-fashion brand owners had no legitimacy for fashion businesses, accustomed to brick-and-mortar distribution and marketing. The new players had to use a different legitimizing rhetoric to develop their early moral legitimacy than the one delivered by fashion industry's most important commercial partners, the retailers. To be sure, even large retailers had various difficulties in attracting high-fashion brands to their online businesses early in 2000s, as recounted by one CEO:

> We were going around to our vendors with whom we do business offline and we were begging them to come to the online channel. I spent my first 12 months crawling and I have bruises on my knees to prove it! There is one story that characterizes the difficulty of getting brands on board. I walked into the president's office of a French fashion company. I showed

him a little PowerPoint presentation and then he wanted to go to the Neiman Marcus website and see for himself. He goes into the search and types YSL (Yves Saint Laurent). And, of course, nothing was supposed to pop up! To my dismay, an YSL handbag pops up on the site. But we were not allowed to sell YSL handbags! As you can imagine, I turned bright red, I packed up my bags and left very quickly. A week later I received a fax, because in 2000, we were actually still receiving fax, and YSL signed on to be a partner with us. They were the first true European luxury brand to come on the store online. As we say, the rest is history.

Despite the mishap, mainstream retailers alluded to the longevity of their relationship with fashion firms as the reason why their clients followed them in the new channel. Their understanding of fashion merchandising that was supposed to be valuable on any channel. Neiman Marcus' CEO reported in 2011 that even though the team "[...] didn't fully understand the power of what we had in our hands [...] this has really become our core competency".

The Director of Marketing in *Digital Moda* explained that when the founders of e-commerce retailers established their ventures they relied on the technical expertise of their founders, who started their careers in online technology pioneers, Amazon and eBay. A co-founder at *Samplemod*—one of the largest e-commerce fashion companies in the United States that specializes in sample sales—explained that her early tenure with eBay influenced the alignment between technical skills and cultural role of her new company:

> I was part of the original team in eBay. I watched it scale from 40 to nearly 5000 when I left. The way this tenure influenced me when I founded [*Samplemod*] was in the use and empowerment of viral marketing. People look at their closet as a collection when shopping on our site in the same way I recognize this happened in terms of emotional connection on eBay. We took from eBay the immediacy of purchase.

Executives in e-commerce frequently showcased their knowledge of fashion by highlighting the desired alignment between their technical skills and projected challenges faced by fashion firms. The North American CEO of *Digital Moda* asserted that:

> If you're talking to fashion companies, they're usually great at developing products but not that great in embracing technologies. But, they are able

to understand the market beyond marketing. What they had forgotten is that their real audiences are customers judging the quality of their product every season. One of our roles is to remind brands of that advocacy.

The Managing Director at *Samplemod* translated their technology skills into a cultural role of "*creators of fashion companies* that *happened to be operating with the aid of* electronic commerce". The Director of Marketing at *Rent-a-Mod* (an e-commerce company specializing in rental high fashion) promoted the role of her organization as a "*cultural* space for experimenting with new *technology* for fashion companies". The co-founder of *Luxemod* accentuated that the skills of her company in e-commerce played important part in the legitimizing process. She frequently referred to the "technical team" in the company as "the brain hub of a *fashion* business". The CEO and founder at *Boutiquemod* (an e-commerce company specializing in acquisition of original next-season high-fashion product) similarly argued that their technology skills were aligned with a distinct cultural role for future fashion partners:

> Technology was the underpinning. From the beginning, we *evolved* from being a *fashion branded shopping site to a marketing channel*. We've created dozens of sales a day and turn inventory more than 70 times a week. We couldn't service [millions of] members without technology. That is a sign of a very interesting business that can never exist offline.

The co-founder of *Luxemod* (one of the largest luxury e-commerce fashion companies online) supported this aggressive approach to moral legitimation. *Luxemod*'s signature proposition was the design of a "shoppable Vogue" space where content was integrated with commerce. The company developed shoppable stylebooks running in 52 weekly issues during the year. This signature element emerged organically, from an experiment ran by the founder, who was in charge of a luxury brick-and-mortar retail business in South America in the 1990s. She noticed that without the Internet, in the early 1990s retailers and small boutique retailers ordered merchandise by flipping through pages of content that merchandising teams in fashion firms had put into look-books before the start of the season. The time lag to order was significant problem for boutiques buying merchandise directly from fashion brands. In this case, clients in her native Venezuela had limited options of viewing this or next year's trends in advance.

In order to be able to show clients look-books for the current season, she started to take pictures of clothes that came in from European fashion houses and send these photographs to her clients, ahead of most European fashion houses' schedule. Excitedly, she noted:

> And, in 1997, the Internet was possible and I started as the founder of companies in E-Commerce. The valuations were crazy. In 1999, the UK connection came to me as a contact via my then-boyfriend. It was my Christmas gift.

Companies that started out the cultural model of sample sales between 2008 and 2009 did benefit from the outstanding inventory that plagued the fashion industry in that period. In New York City, *Samplemod* was founded as a viable distribution channel for brands lacking liquidation strategies for their excess product between 2007 and 2009. One of the co-founders at *Samplemod* had previously worked as a merchandiser for luxury brands and spent 90% of her job finding the brands and talking to them. The first brands positioned for sample sale were based on "networks of friends that we had relationships with. These first brands were considered by the fashion public to be highly coveted [and]... Those set the bar high and reflected on the kind of brand that we were developing".

Samplemod exploited the aspiration of consumers for discounted branded fashion product, available exclusively "by invitation only". Each day at 12 p.m. *Samplemod* started an online sale of limited volume of merchandise with only a few brands. The search for moral legitimacy was aggressive. "We take the merchandise risk", explained one co-founder.

> We buy and we do consignment. We just take delivery about a month later. We know the amount of available inventory; we shop samples; we host the sale and then, once we know how much we sell, we say to our partner: okay, send us 1320 items of the product, for example.

Using this narrative line and method of acquisition, in 2010 *Samplemod* hosted 17 sales daily, for 36 hours, and had a total of 750 brands serviced. This was a 100-brand increase from 2007. At the height of the financial meltdown between 2008–2010, 92% of merchandise on *Samplemod* was sold out consistently and the user membership increased from zero in 2007 to 2,500,000 members in 2010. Over 50,000 brand items were moving out of distribution centers weekly. This represented a tremendous amount of throughput given the short time window during which sales were hosted.

According to the executive team, founders at *Samplemod* discovered fairly swiftly that their aggressive legitimation approach apparently tapped into new sources of value for fashion brands. Despite the fact that this was a deeply discounted channel, established fashion brands began to warm up to aggressive narratives for legitimization detailing the argument that fashion firms lacked young customer base for their future. Zac Posen, the brand started by the eponymous US designer, was one of *Samplemod*'s first clients. Zac Posen's brand was young and flexible and these characteristics helped make the sale proposition work. The exposure was successful and in the 6-months period between December 1, 2009 and June 11, 2010, Zac Posen was featured three times: January 5th, April 3rd, and June 1st, 2009. Another contemporary fashion brand featured early in the history of *Samplemod* was Michael Kors, whose eponymous KORS Ltd., launched in 2004, is known for its flexibility to channel collaboration. "*We are reinterpreting these brands for a younger generation*", one co-founder argued; asserting that the point for legitimation was that *Samplemod*'s business model was there to stay.

After 2010, as fashion product cycles stabilized, one co-founder argued that the technical skills of the company aligned with a wholly different cultural role that could not be performed by actors in the brick-and-mortar domain:

> What we realized around three-four months in, is that most companies work with us not necessarily or exclusively by any stretch of the imagination because they had inventory they had to clear; because they didn't have outlets; or, because they did not have appropriate outlets, but they started working with us because *they realized almost before we did*, that *we are an effective marketing channel* to reach new customers.

Aside from showcasing how e-commerce technology can help fashion companies engage in new commercial and aesthetic activities, in seeking moral legitimacy e-commerce fashion companies also incorporated in their narratives that they understood existing practices and values in fashion companies. E-commerce and social commerce companies argued that their expertise in curation would embody both economic and aesthetic advantages for fashion firms. Founders at *Luxemod* and *Digidesigner*, as well in *StyleMag* and *CommunityMag*, asserted that the knowledge of their online merchandisers in curating fashion product that is browsed and shopped by a community of consumers was a new functional advantage that could not be performed in the brick-and-mortar field.

"I definitely think of myself as an editor", a co-founder at *Luxemod* maintained. "A fashion retailer *thinks* as an *editor*", the co-founder at *Digidesigner* noted prescriptively. Merchandising executives at *Luxemod* formalized this narrative by developing an edition of fifty-two online magazine issues on their website that curated luxury fashion product, shoppable on a click. "We have to consider", the co-founder argued, that "*content and commerce are fused together*. It would take you a good afternoon to go and check out a department store. Editing is perhaps the most important thing you can do".

At *Digidesigner*, the two co-founders engaged in what they called building legitimacy by advocacy. In their narratives, they considered the role of their company as 'a fashion incubator platform', inviting consumers to support emerging designers by backing financially their future collections. In meetings with fashion companies, founders offered advocacy that disavowed the value of relationships fashion companies had built with fashion magazines. "I mean, just in terms of what is happening in these worlds", argued one co-founder,

> They are losing power by the minute. There is this famous quote by Suzy Menkez: '2009 is the first year when fashion became a conversation'. That was in front of me. That Vogue or Elle have less of a say in purchases. So, blogs like Fashionista – they actually drive a lot of purchase behavior. Over 50 per cent of purchases online are made with a trigger from a blog. So, for me, to be [formally] trained in editorials becomes less and less important.

The approach of *Digital Moda* and its peers to enabling institutional change in the industry was through their strategic use of rhetoric (Suddaby and Greenwood 2005). On the road to moral legitimacy, *Digital Moda* engaged in the development of elaborate *narratives for legitimization*, intended for fashion companies. These were symbolic resources that offered, as per *Digital Moda*'s CTE, an "alternative" vision to fashion companies and to the fashion industry. The role of *Digital Moda* and peers in digital fashion was to defuse opposing conceptions harbored by fashion companies on the role of e-commerce in fashion. The goal, instead, was to connect the two competing fields—the technical field in which Digital Moda was operating and the institutional field in which fashion companies were embedded. "This was it", the CTE asserted, "[our role was to] *effectively bridge these two ways,* because fashion is an industry very driven by relationships and not necessarily beta products, which you find in technology". The Director of Marketing fleshed out the narrative as an attempt to influence fashion companies in accepting new practices where

> The Internet might be a game changer. We were not exactly generating the change, because market effects and technology generated the change. But, *maybe the possibility was there to helping the change to become real.* We set out to help fashion companies understand that change is occurring and how to face it. The point is not telling them how to replicate on the web what they already have. The point is to be the global Internet partner for these firms.

The Director of Communications at a luxury European fashion company provided an example of the degree of cultural support for narratives for legitimization of *Digital Moda, Samplemod,* and *StyleMag:*

> I definitely think that [*Digital Moda*] have become key point of reference for decision-makers. I definitely think it's a problem if you are not there. Technically, I will not make money in that channel, but for the purpose of the image of the brand, I am willing to be there; I am even willing to pay to be there.

For social commerce companies, the road to institutional legitimacy was more difficult. In their latest iteration, as emerging members of the domain of digital fashion, social commerce companies were seeking to combine the business model of PCEs with the expansion of purely editorial content around fashion. Companies, such as *StyleMag* developed proprietary search algorithms that filtered the latest fashion brands, styles, and retailers with dedicated editorial content. The founder of *StyleMag*—Internet's largest company in social commerce—argued that the institutional value of the model is to be "a *fashion search engine.* We are the largest fashion search engine globally: US, UK, Germany, and France; we recently launched in Japan. We have about 7 million monthly unique users and we actually drive traffic to retailers and brands. The transaction itself happens on the retailer site. Think of it as *Google for fashion*".

The CEO of *StyleMag* conceptualized the collaboration between social commerce and e-commerce fashion companies as key ingredient to discovering new sources of aesthetic and commercial value for fashion brands. The executive noted that collaborating with peers was actually *as important as trying to sign on individual fashion labels.* For social commerce players, negotiating with e-commerce fashion companies allowed to acquire contextual knowledge about fashion companies with which the former had no direct relationship.

> One of the things that we found effective is collaborating with others. Or maybe someone has audience that doesn't know [us] or people were using [us] do not know the partners brand very well. So, we're doing contests and collaborations. One of the recent contest and collaborations we did was with Diane von Furstenberg, *Tablet* Hotels and [*Digital Moda*]. So, we brought these three groups of fans together. Let everybody sort of touch each other and bring everybody together.

The goal of social commerce players was to convince e-commerce fashion companies and their fashion brand partners that unlike fashion magazines, where partners turn to relations of pure display advertising, the collaborations here created a new form of *marketing by involvement.* As the cultural field evolved, it became more important to integrate narratives for legitimization of e-commerce and social commerce players. Because of the ambiguity of their earlier PCE function, fashion firms had found it difficult to accept social commerce companies as editors of branded fashion content. Very few fashion companies were early adopters of social commerce. One of these early pioneer fashion companies, a large European-born fashion brand represented by its Marketing Director, considered the pairing of content and fashion product offered by social commerce to become an important cultural tool for fashion brands in the future and change the way fashion brands perceived the sources of its own brand value.

> It is valuable to communicate with people through content, to build community through content. There is a lot of value of driving this activity off-site - where the community is - and drive them to the website, as opposed to try to make everybody to come to E-Commerce to partake. So, we try to get people from Facebook or twitter or *StyleMag* where they *already are*, to come to our website.

Social commerce companies took advantage of growing customer inter-action with fashion content, igniting large audiences to visit custom-de-veloped look-books, trend reports, blogs, and fan pages. Some social commerce companies, most notably, *StyleMag* generated and curated over 10 million products from more than 14,000 partner blogs and e-commerce retailers, brick-and-mortar department stores with digital divisions, and even with established fashion brands. Social commerce companies subsequently introduced editorial and social community com-ponents as part of their institutional legitimacy package by linking users to a highly curated ecology of fashion content linked to e-commerce fashion retail websites. "I think we were pretty early in the Social Media space", the founder of *StyleMag* related; "when we launched in 2004, we came in together with *both* social commerce *and search*. We are a con-tent and commerce company. The goal is to curate content such that it is more findable".

The emergence of social search as a new function in social commerce companies has shed the liability of their past association with PCE func-tionality and augmented their partnership with e-commerce fashion companies. An example of this institutional approach is Polyvore.com—a community-centered social commerce company that empowers users to build "sets" by pairing brands pinned by users into outfits and aggregat-ing similar sets into style galleries, where each product in a set is clickable and buyable (Fig. 2.1).

Users discover brands by tapping into Polyvore's extensive product range, generated by Polyvore when tapping into the product feeds of its e-commerce partners. The company has developed an interface that seamlessly integrates between the difficult work on ensuring that its user community appreciates the aesthetics in the presentation of fashion sets, curated by users, and guaranteeing that said sets would be marketable. Brand awareness campaigns endorsed by fashion companies are also a frequent captivator of user audiences. Such campaigns rely on the com-mentary and judgment of fashion "influencers" and contemporary fash-ion designers, such as Prabal Gurung, CEO of the eponymous label, who have frequently participated in judging branded contests, choosing among the many user-generated looks those with substantive curative appeal. User participation in these branded contests is encouraged by the promise of either receiving tickets to a designer's fashion show or touring their studio.

POLYVORE   Shop   Ask   Explore   Create

Up & Coming Sets

Fig. 2.1   Polyvore.com—building "sets"

As a result of developing social search, since 2010, e-commerce companies (such as *Digital Moda, Luxemod,* and *Samplemod*) have seen even deeper engagement with social commerce companies (such as *StyleMag* and *CommunityMag*) in representing their fashion company clients. Social commerce partners have, obviously, been enthusiastic at the prospect of gaining further legitimacy with fashion companies, wary of their previous status. "We do see that when it comes to [E-Commerce fashion] retailers", offered *StyleMag*'s CEO, in an attempt to demonstrate an alignment between *StyleMag*'s social commerce goals and those of e-commerce partners, "some of them are very good editorially and in terms of the content they provide. *Digital Moda* and *Luxemod,* for example, one of their core principles is to unite the two functions of magazine and shopping. You see high conversions from retailers doing just that".

FORMALIZING COMMERCIAL PRACTICE INTO PRAGMATIC LEGITIMACY

By 2010, e-commerce fashion companies in this analysis had established direct commercial practice with the merchandising departments of fashion companies in USA and Europe and their buying teams consistently acquired current season merchandise. As these organizations gained cultural support and were pushed into the mainstream arena of fashion, their executives developed and formalized new practices by working with social commerce companies. Co-branding was introduced as a new practice to fashion partner companies in a series of meetings between with the Global Director of Buying at *Digital Moda* between 2011 and 2012. *Digital Moda* secured an increasing number of fashion companies for which to develop and run e-commerce websites and the executive team in the US office began to push the idea in meetings with fashion companies that their fashion product online should be made widely available *outside* of their own e-commerce website. The Global Director of Buying at *Digital Moda* considered both the commercial and aesthetic component of such a move:

> In the end of the day, content becomes essential, because the only way for us to reinstate or reinforce the idea to fashion companies that whether it is a video, behind the scenes – you are constantly telling a story, you're constantly branding. A brand needs to give a little bit more than just its product. And the brands have seen the numbers. It's that simple.

In a meeting with the Creative Director and Merchandisers in one fashion company, the North American CEO at *Digital Moda* explained that the intent of collaboration between e-commerce and social commerce companies was to make "fashion more relevant" both as economic and aesthetic activity in the e-commerce arena. The CEO argued that the goal of extending the online presence of fashion companies was directly related to developing influence legitimacy; effectively, as a special form of pragmatic legitimacy. "*Our practice* directly influences how established fashion companies approach the online channel", he noted, "[because] online technology has expanded the social function of the Internet and *moves the point of purchase and aligns it with the point of advertising*".

Digital Moda eventually gained explicit sanction from fashion brands to link selected fashion product from a fashion company's e-commerce website directly to social commerce partners. This provided impetus to formalize the emerging practice of Co-branding in commercial agreements. Directors of Marketing in *Digital Moda, Luxemod,* and *Samplemod* approached founders in *StyleMag* and *CommunityMag* to explore how complementarities in technology can impart commercial value and derive further cultural acceptance from fashion brands.

Digital Moda developed Co-branding with *StyleMag* and *CommunityMag,* the largest social commerce companies in online fashion. Both types of organizations had overt responsibility for formalizing the steps constitutive of developing the practice. *Digital Moda* was responsible for building a shopping webpage (called 'e-shoplet') hosted on the counterpart's social commerce webpage. Online buyers and merchandisers in *Digital Moda* were also responsible for curating the selection of fashion product to be displayed in these campaigns. The social commerce counterpart chose weekly themes for collaboration. The curated fashion galleries were displayed and promoted for a limited time as "look of the week" and "limited edition looks". The Director of Marketing in *Digital Moda* noted how both online partners to a curation agreement had autonomy in choosing themes and curated products for a campaign:

> In the beginning of each month, our partners choose the editorial looks they want us to curate. They say: 'you guys know best what items you have as long as you make sure you align with the look.' They will send us the desired looks and we will go out and look for products [from our fashion partners] that are similar to the desired. And, we will publish that on their web-store. This mini-shoplet is [...] not only curated, but also *controlled* by us [...]. If this brand sells out next week, it will automatically be changed by another product with a similar look, which we've already chosen to put in the system.

Fashion editors at PaperMag returned the legitimating sentiment by indicating that the longevity of the relationship was determined by the ability of partners, like *Digital Moda,* to surprise them with styles for each weekly theme throughout the year: "We always try to stump them; one week we gave them a still from The African Queen, but sure enough they supplied us with lots of Victorian lace collar shirts and khaki button downs. They've got everything!"

The evolution of Co-branding collaboration between e-commerce and social commerce companies indicated the growing pragmatic legitimacy of online fashion organizations with fashion companies, because the latter had to agree to be featured in such a campaign. The Director of Marketing at *Digital Moda* described the importance to legitimize *Co-branding* as a "reinvention of curation" for fashion companies. The transformation of this practice for the digital age was significant. In the past, the definition of curation has been that of an "officer in charge of a museum, gallery of art, library, or the like[3]" who had full "responsibility for the production, interpretation, and dissemination of cultural productions" (DiMaggio and Useem 1978, p. 359). Amateur-curators have now supplanted this critical function in this creative industry. Co-branding supported and further promoted the role of e-commerce and social commerce organizations as guardians of new aesthetic and commercial values for fashion firms.

Extending Pragmatic Legitimacy into Influence Legitimacy, and the 'Culture Premium'

Between 2011 and 2012, e-commerce companies expanded the type and frequency of long-term Curation agreements with fashion companies and accepted a variety of explicit curating responsibilities within the scope of these agreements (Fig. 2.2).

The terms of agreements itemized the growing responsibilities of e-commerce partners. Marketing Directors in e-commerce companies typically settled on two types of curation campaigns. The first option was to showcase "deeper" selection across categories from a *single* fashion brand. An example of this approach is shown in Fig. 2.3, which presents a typical e-commerce design of a curation campaign, in this case between Moda Operandi (e-commerce company) and Marchesa (a fashion company).

The other approach was to feature "highly curated" e-commerce boutiques from a variety of luxury brands several times throughout the year, but have one primary collaborating fashion brand to sponsor the exclusive selection of brands. An example is the editorial and product collaboration *"101 Trends"*, featuring curated looks and video content (Fig. 2.4), created by Net-a-Porter (e-commerce fashion company) and sponsored by Chloé (French luxury fashion house). For the fashion

Curaton Agreements
with fashion brands.

•Co-developing onlinemarketing
campaigns
•Curating "representative" product
•Curating product from co-located
brands

Fig. 2.2   Extending pragmatic legitimacy with fashion companies

PRE-FALL 2015
MARCHESA
TRUNKSHOW ENDING IN 7 DAYS.

The New York designers channel fabergé eggs with
ornate embroideries and lavish fabrics. Intricate
metallic embellishments gild frothy swathes of
tulle and lace, evoking a regal romance that
celebrates the era. A range of dramatic silhouettes
drapes the female form with 17th-century
opulence.

M'OST WANTED VIEW ALL M'OST WANTED ▸

Cap Sleeve Sequin Mermaid Gown	Sequin And Threadwork Organza Cocktail Dress	Tiered Tulle Gown	Embroidered V-Neck Long Sleeve Tulle Gown	Corded Lace Cocktail Dress
$5,295	$2,995	$6,995 ($3,498	$10,950	$3,995 ($1,998

Fig. 2.3   Co-branding—Moda Operandi and Marchesa

company, this collaborative editorial approach was cheaper in relation to
the high cost associated with opening a brand-specific e-commerce presence. A related advantage was that the fashion company demonstrated
that it relied on the emerging moral and pragmatic legitimacy of the
'host' platform; in this case, Net-a-Porter.

In *Digital Moda*, the approach to expanding pragmatic legitimacy
involved an additional structural component—the institutionalization of

Fig. 2.4 Editorial collaboration—"in association with Chloé"

two new organizational units, *Partner Division* in 2006, and *Pure Brand Unit*[4] in 2010. The North American CEO put it succinctly: "*The website is to E-Commerce what the store was to retail 10 years ago.* Your own website is the most powerful communication tool you can have to the global consumer". The objective of the first unit was to influence the formation of e-commerce teams in fashion companies, created and supported by *Digital Moda*. The second unit, as per the North American CEO, who became vital agent for this approach, was to "directly *influence* the *cultural architectures* of fashion brands". He noted that, "because most of the brands are still 'children', we are starting out slowly". Fashion partners of *Digital Moda* for which the company had built e-commerce properties, did not have digital teams in 2010, and *Pure Brand Unit* had to convince their merchandising and communication teams to add other digital marketing activities on top of e-commerce.

As the objective expanded to *influence* the direction of strategy for fashion companies, the terms of curation agreements expanded and a new tactic that helped influence legitimacy was developed. The tactic can be formulated as a set of concessions on the part of e-commerce companies (a 'culture premium'), in which fashion company partners opt into assuming a measure of "creative control" (CEO, *Samplemod*) over the design of co-branded campaigns, as well as control over the look and feel of photography, models, and makeup. *Samplemod* is a good case in point for understanding how the 'culture premium' works. The company started out as a discounted marketing channel, but by the end of the financial crisis, in 2011, the founding team decided to offer premium coverage for certain costs to fashion brand partners, to offset differences in culture and solicit their participation in the experiment of being featured online.

One co-founder at *Samplemod* explained that fashion brands became interested in curation, when merchandisers in the company decided to offer "full creative control" to editors and merchandisers in partner fashion brands, in areas related to photography, models, makeup, and editorials; all produced with explicit agreement from the brand. "It felt as if, organically, from the beginning, our culture emerged," explained one co-founder. "We firmly believed in brand building with [fashion companies]. I felt, kind of like, together building brand equity". Fashion brand partners appreciated the gesture. As indicated by fashion executives, the principal costs in fashion firms are related to production, marketing, and distribution. Within this predicament, costs that could not be reduced, as per the CIO at *MilanModa1* were *"marketing* costs, [because] publicity, and advertising do follow some rules". Similarly, per the Head of Global Communications at *MilanModa3*, "ad costs are a big issue; we spend a lot on real model photography". Having these particular costs covered was vital for the future relationship. A final concession from *Samplemod* was inherent in the business model of the company; the creation of exclusive space for registered customers only. According to one executive, these selective concessions were beneficial to developing influence legitimacy:

> Our brand partners work with us because they love the way we are featuring their brand; investing in photography; keeping *true to their image*. They love the fact that it is a private area for a members-only audience. We just had our first sale with [a luxury fashion brand], and when it's over, nobody can know what merchandise was on the site, how much of it was sold, etc. The site doesn't say – and that is by design, exactly how many [pieces] are currently available for purchase or what season it was designed for.

The development of the 'culture premium' was a tactic aimed at extending pragmatic legitimacy into influence legitimacy in curation agreements with fashion companies. *Digital Moda*, the UK-born *Luxemod*, and the North American *Samplemod* and *Boutiquemod* used the culture premium to eventually gain status as commercial partners of fashion companies and, subsequently, to place merchandise orders alongside large retailers at the beginning of product cycles. As the moral and pragmatic legitimacy of e-commerce and social commerce companies grew, their executives began communicating curation choices to fashion brand partners with increasing authority, indicative of an evolution in their influence. Terse notations were frequently used, such as, "we were taken with their trend"(co-founder, *Luxemod*), and "we should be very open to include new brands, because variety is our value" (founder, *Boutiquemod*). The Managing Director at *Samplemod* ultimately asserted *Samplemod* offered fashion companies "the *privilege* of being exposed to new audiences. They love the way we are featuring their brand; investing in photography; keeping *true to their image*". The co-founder of *Luxemod* argued, "we have a voice that we believe is *the voice of authority* in terms of what the categories out there are that we can translate to the digital channel".

The Director of Marketing at *Digital Moda* USA approved of concessions as an important "first step in the direction of *strategic branding* with fashion labels". The Global Director of Marketing further established the value of the approach—"this is why we never promote [*Digital Moda*] as a *service provider*. What we do is enable fashion companies [to] understand how change is occurring and how to face it". To enrich the prestige and power of *Digital Moda* in the fashion arena, the US Director of Marketing exploited the advantage of having numerous fashion partners:

> Having so many fashion partners gives us a lot of power [...]. We are now in a position to tell our brands: look, we now have long-term partnerships with these companies, and work like an agency. So, if you're interested in having a curative digital partnership with them, we have the knowledge. This is a good position for us. We can say to them [companies] in return; when you partner with us, you actually partner with our fashion partners.

An added element of influence legitimacy was to position oneself as an emerging new cultural arbiter in the industry. *Luxemod*'s CEO put it this way—

> Young brands are very keen on getting on [*Luxemod*]. We get hundreds of emails from new brands. Use a catchy subject phrase and attach a great picture presentation of your product". [*Luxemod*] doesn't have set rules on what brands are going to be part of our content and product portfolio. The young brand has to tell us how it is different than the other brands, because we are always interested in telling the story of the brand. *In a way, think about how you would pitch to a magazine.*

The growing influence legitimacy was manifest in the shifting positions of fashion brands with regard to which companies they saw as partners and competitors. The Vice President of e-commerce at a luxury fashion label in the United States argued that, "as global as the brand is, I have many *competitors* and *partners* that I deal with—Saks, Neiman, *Luxemod*". The acquisition of influence legitimacy was also evident in formal statements made by e-commerce founders in popular media and at industry meetings on the importance of their contribution to the future of fashion. The co-founder in charge of merchandising at *Samplemod* frequently contributed a variant of the following account: "If you go to a department store, you will see their selection for the fall. It is now July and nobody wants to buy a cashmere sweater. They want to buy something out of a box and they throw on immediately. So, we are selling Spring-Summer merchandise, which to a shopper is current; Department store is one season old". An executive at *Luxemod* offered an identical value statement, "you go at a department store right now and what is available is mohair sweater. You go in September and there is huge consumer frenzy on the Internet but none of the product is available for the next 6 months".

In fact, as influential players, companies such as *Digital Moda* and *Luxemod* interpreted the value of their cultural contribution to be equivalent or even superior to that of traditional partners of fashion companies, Vogue and Neiman Marcus. An oft-repeated statement signaling the production of influence legitimacy was that fashion brands had "lost exclusivity" that can only be reenacted by skipping a fashion season. Said one of the co-founders of *Luxemod*:

> We skip a season. It will give all designers a break and next September, instead of spring shows, the designers show the fall shows and get the products to stores few years later. And, then, the buyers and the editors, *we* just do our jobs and go behind and procure the stuff. *We are all very capable to say what is new and important without the wait.* We don't need to see the show.

Advocating for skipping of a season was in line with ideas expressed in the industry. Although an enduring practice, seasonal fashion shows had gradually left the industry threadbare with the arrival of e-commerce, digital runways, and 'seasonless' collections, such as in 2012 by Stefano Pilati, former Head of Design at *Ermenegildo Zegna* for *Agnona*, the womenswear complement to *Zegna* (Mau 2013). In 2013, Diane von Furstenberg, chairwoman of the Council of Fashion Designers of America (CFDA), announced that, "someday designers might show their collections only digitally" (Chrisman-Campbell 2016). In 2016, *Burberry* reported that after September, seasonless men's and women's collections will be displayed twice a year on the runway, and, following their début will be directly available in store and on its e-commerce front (Conti 2016).

Influence legitimacy indicated to industry insiders that the objective of new institutional entrepreneurs in e-commerce was to create new fashion elites in the emerging institutional field of digital fashion. Legitimacy narratives had rotated on their axis. Executives at *Samplemod* conferred around tactics for "giving brands visibility and credibility". Their colleagues at *Luxemod* announced that fashion brands must "keep their brand really hot", if they desire that their product be acquired and featured on *Luxemod*. Personal stories became mythologized and important in promoting the clout of these new fashion industry players. A close relative of one of *Luxemod*'s co-founders had at one point suggested contracting one of France's oldest luxury fashion brands to be featured on the company's roster of fashion brands. The merchandising team, however, decided that they "did not think that the brand was actually right for *Luxemod*". Ultimately, the brand's merchandise was acquired a few months later, indicating that the rhetorical value of these statements was to boost influence legitimacy.

Narratives are important in establishing new elite culture for the fashion industry in the new institutional field of digital fashion. The new players are unencumbered by historic cultural rites of conduct laid out by established brand-making partners from the recent past. Their founders attempt to understand and reinterpret the fashion industry for the digital age. "I am not sure that any of the rules have been written yet", indicated the former CEO of *Luxemod*. "We are unpredictable and change our minds all the time".

The Head of Global Communications at the Italian luxury fashion brand *MilanModa3* summed up her conceptualization for the importance of emerging players as new cultural "branding" elites:

> The old audiences were OK because you only gave them the clothes that you produced. These guys *want and require something special*. I certainly would love to engage with all of these but I think we can only go to these channels, if we have something special to offer them and their clients. I don't think we can go to them with the regular collection, which you can find in any other store or a multi-brand store, such as Neiman Marcus.

NOTES

1. Part of this chapter was reproduced from Petkova, I 2016, 'Between high-tech and high-fashion: How e-commerce fashion organizations gain moral and pragmatic legitimacy in the fashion field', *Poetics*, Vol. 57 (August 2016), Pages 55–69. The main focus of my empirical study is *Digital Moda*, complemented with interviews with other e-commerce companies

(*Luxemod, Samplemod, Boutiquemod, Digidesign, Rent-a-mod*) and social commerce companies (*StyleMag, CommunityMag*). Names of organizations from my empirical study featured in Table 2.1 are pseudonyms. Details of organizations, branded websites, and projects are deliberately vague to disguise identities.

2. Chief Executive Officer (CEO) at *StyleMag* in an interview.
3. Hunter Diary LVIII. 42 The Curators of the British Musæum, 1767, Oxford English Dictionary.
4. The names of *Partner Division* and *Pure Brand Unit* divisions are pseudonyms.

BIBLIOGRAPHY

Bluefly, Inc. (2001). *Form 10-K* Annual Report *2001*. Retrieved from: SEC EDGAR website http://www.sec.gov/edgar.shtml. [25 May 2017].

Bluefly, Inc. (2002). *Form 10-K* Annual Report *2000*. Retrieved from: SEC EDGAR website http://www.sec.gov/edgar.shtml. [25 May 2017].

Bluefly, Inc. (2011). *Form 10-K* Annual Report *2000*. Retrieved from: SEC EDGAR website http://www.sec.gov/edgar.shtml. [25 May 2017].

Bluefly, Inc. (2012). *Form 10-K* Annual Report *2000*. Retrieved from: SEC EDGAR website http://www.sec.gov/edgar.shtml. [25 May 2017].

Brohan, M. (2006). Pure-play web retailers have 54% more visits than multi-channel retailers. *Internet Retailer*. Retrieved may 7, 2018 from https://www.digitalcommerce360.com/2006/12/27/pure-play-web-retailers-have-54-more-visits-than-multi-channel/.

Chi, E.H. (2009). Information seeking can be social. *Computer, 3*, 42–46.

Chrisman-Campbell, K. (2016). Is this the end for fashion week? *The Atlantic*. Retrieved from: https://www.theatlantic.com/entertainment/archive/2016/02/the-end-of-the-runway/461862/. [26 June 2017].

Conti, S. (2016). Burberry's bold move: To make shows direct to consumer. *Women's Wear Daily (WWD.com)*. Retrieved from: http://wwd.com/fashion-news/designer-luxury/burberry-runway-delivery-schedule-direct-consumer-10340340/. [26 June 2017].

Cronin, A.M. (2004). Regimes of mediation, advertising practitioners as cultural intermediaries? *Consumption Markets & Culture, 7*(4), 349–369.

DiMaggio, P.J., & Powell, W.W. (1983). The iron cage revisited, Institutional isomorphism & collective rationality in organizational fields. *American Sociological Review, 48*, 147–160.

DiMaggio, P.J., & Useem, M. (1978). Cultural property & public policy: Emerging tensions in government support for the arts. *Social Research, 45*(2), 356–389.

Laudon, K.C., & Traver, G.G. (2003). *E-Commerce, business, technology and society*. Addison Wesley, 2nd edition.

Mau, D. (2013). *Stefano Pilati bucks fashion cycle with 'seasonless' debut Agnona collection*. Fashionista.com. Retrieved from: https://fashionista.com/2013/09/stefano-pilati-bucks-fashion-cycle-with-seasonless-debut-agnona-collection. [26 June 2017].

Meyer, J.W., & Scott, W.R. (1983). Centralization and the legitimacy problems of local Government. In Meyer, J.W., & Scott, W.R. (Eds.), *Organizational environments: Ritual and rationality*. Newbury Park: Sage.

NOWNESS. (2017). *About us: A global video channel screening the best in culture*. Retrieved from: https://www.nowness.com/about. [26 June 2017].

Powell, W.W. (2012a). Expanding the scope of institutional analysis. In DiMaggio, P.J., & Powell, W.W. (Eds.), *The new institutionalism in organizational analysis*, 183–201, Chicago, IL: University of Chicago Press.

Powell, W.W. (2012b). The organization of societal sectors, propositions and early evidence. In Powell, W.W., & DiMaggio, P.J. (Eds.), *The new institutionalism in organizational analysis*. Chicago, IL: University of Chicago Press.

PRWeb. (2009). LVMH-owned eLUXURY closing down retail operations. *Cision PRWeb*. Retrieved from: http://www.prweb.com/releases/2009/06/prweb2487254.htm. [26 June 2017].

Suddaby, R., & Greenwood, R. (2005). Rhetorical strategies of legitimacy. *Administrative Science Quarterly, 50*(1), 35–67.

Walmsley, A. (2008). *Web should be in the lap of luxury*. Factiva.com. Retrieved from: http://luxuryinstitute.com/graphics/doclib/2008/Marketing8208LI.pdf. [25 June 2017].

Zhu, K. (2004). The complementarity of information technology infrastructure & E-Commerce capability: A resource-based assessment of their business value. *Journal of Management Information Systems, 21*(1), 167–202.

CHAPTER 3

Fashion Companies: Organizational Responses to Managing Innovation in E-Commerce Practice

For the Italian shop, online retail is just another store. *We never moved to the next level to think that the online store is actually something completely different...* It is something broader; needs more.... more activities... different activities, than a regular store...

—CIO, *MilanModal.*

"The most important thing about organizations"—Selznick has reminded us—"is that, though they are tools, each nevertheless has a life of its own" (Selznick 1949, p. 10). The process through which established fashion companies undertook changes in their organizations related to e-commerce begins with a review of the institutionalized divides existing in the structure of these creative organizations between functions associated with 'aesthetics' and 'commerce'. The response to change in fashion companies exposes the enduring practice of institutionalized organizations to maintain organizational structures that are only loosely related to work repertoires, and, instead, are closely related to established rhetoric and ritual (Meyer and Rowan 1977; Powell 2012). One of the earliest and most influential conceptions that explain how change occurs in organizations is Selznick's idea that "'to institutionalize' means *to infuse with value* beyond the technical requirements of the task at hand" (2011, p. 17, original emphasis) Meyer and Rowan (1977) originally explained institutionalization as a tool for compliance, used by organizations in a field to alleviate tensions between 'saying' and 'doing'. Since organizational structure is a reaction response to pressures from the external environment along with

© The Author(s) 2018
I. Petkova, *Engineering Legitimacy,*
https://doi.org/10.1007/978-3-319-90707-9_3

commitments by participants (Scott 2008), organizations are likely to adopt functions or roles in response to institutional demands, but then 'decouple' these from actual practices. Current neo-institutional research (Edelman 1992; Zajac and Westphal 1994) has further found that decoupling structure from everyday work varies among organizations, depending on field and industry. Nevertheless, we know little about the actual processes that established organizations in creative fields undergo, when deciding on what new practices to create and how to implement them, upon accepting pressures from the external environment or internal participants.

The decoupling of formal structure from actual work is an important chunk in the decision-making apparatus of incumbent fashion companies. In fact, over time, executives in fashion companies have constructed fissures between the formal structure and actual work practice to manage one of the most significant relationships in fashion—balancing between aesthetic and commercial practice. Work repertoires in fashion companies are produced through "negotiations between the interests of [various] collective actors (manufacturers and media, above all) and [...] individual actors" (Mora 2006, p. 335). Professional fashion organizations and practitioners in fashion—companies, retail consultancies, flagship associations, designers, advertising, and publishing agencies—take advantage of the division between aesthetic and commercial practices. Aspers and Godart have conceptualized this metaphoric representation of organizational reality as a "tension between art and commerce" (2013, p. 180). Executives in merchandising, retailing, and advertising, for example, are tied up in a commercial enterprise (Aspers and Godart 2013). Creative teams, communications directors, and head designers, instead, have traditionally influenced the trajectory of aesthetic direction in fashion firms.

In recent years, however, the symbolic boundaries that have traditionally separated aesthetic and economic labor in fashion companies have become increasingly porous (Petkova 2016). Evidence for a convergence between artistic rhetoric and actual work repertoires has surfaced only in recent years, congruently with the emergence of new institutional entrepreneurs and organizational models in digital fashion. In 2006, Mora highlighted that fashion practitioners working outside design, such as visual merchandisers producing "forms of creativity that are *different* from designers and communicators" (p. 349, emphasis added) had acquired growing influence in fashion firms. In 2014, Pedroni and Volonté noted that Milanese designers have started to emphasize a "culture of wearability" (2014, p. 110), in which art gives way to the service relation of apparel in their practice. Also in 2014, Van De Peer had documented that a counterintuitive move had taken hold in fashion journalism. It appeared that to compensate for the growing importance of commercial practice in fashion companies, fashion journalists have started to reinterpret fashion as an intellectual practice.

These examples show that in recent years that as an institutional field, the fashion industry has entered a process in which the contested cultural worlds of commercial and artistic production have become tangled. Shapiro and Heinich (2012) have termed this adaptation process as 'intermittent artification' of a cultural field. Intermittent artification is an outcome from various institutional pressures affecting the field, such as organizational change, or legal consolidation (e.g., the loss of artistic autonomy by fashion designers to international financial conglomerates). Working in an industry where aesthetic and commercial discourse is intertwined and products "[...] return for a while to the world of ritual, and then re-enter the art system and be redefined as museum pieces" (2012, p. 11), involves substantial amount of boundary work for fashion company executives, who are forced to repeatedly restructure their roles in the formal structure as these relate to actual work.

As e-commerce companies continue establishing moral and pragmatic legitimacy in the fashion field, both parts of the process comprising 'intermittent' artification have been observed inside fashion companies: *de-artification* or *re-artification*. De-artification emerges when fashion companies are narrowing the gap between formal organizational structure and actual work practice in an attempt to acquire efficiency and safeguard legitimacy in the emerging field of digital fashion (Table 3.1). In some of the cases outlined in this book, a further expression of de-artification is observed, called 'resistance to artification' (Shapiro and Heinich 2012). This institutional alignment occurs when executives representing new units in the formal structure of fashion companies begin to further deemphasize the nature of their work from dominant narratives of artistic discourse, such as appreciation for the symbolic value of the fashion product that eclipses its material properties (Bourdieu and Delsaut 1975). Resistance to artification can be validated by observing subtle changes emerging in the practice of fashion companies, most notably associated with a reshaping of the roles and identities of executives, "such that officers become internal advocates for reforms, both procedural and substantive" (Scott 2008, p. 432). In short, resistance to artification in fashion companies occurs when, in response to institutional pressures, new and existing executives are consistently championing the formation of new units in which perceptions about the formal organizational structure *and* the content of practice are aligned.

Table 3.1   Re-artification and de-artification as institutional practices

Process	Material practice	Organizational actors[a]
De-artification Closing of the gap between formal organizational structure and actual work practice	**Resistance to artification** De-emphasis from narratives of artistic discourse • Combines commercial and aesthetic rhetoric (e.g., in *BritModa*, examples of these practices are 'engagement and performance' and 'revenue-driven branding') • Roles and identities of existing/new executives are reshaped such that executives become internal advocates for reforms	New executives; new organizational units in the formal structure Web Editor (*MilanModa1*) Head Global Communications (*MilanModa3*) Head Global Digital Marketing (*MilanModa3*) Head Social Media (*MilanModa3*) VP Global Marketing (*BritModa*) Director Social Media (*BritModa*) VP Media Planning (*BritModa*) Director Digital Marketing (*Maison Française*) Project Manager e-commerce (*Maison Française*)
Re-artification Maintaining the gap between formal organizational structure and actual work practice	**Ritual practice** Continued emphasis on narratives of artistic discourse despite structural or procedural changes (such as new organizational units, introduction of new practice) • Planned or intended new material practice is introduced, but obfuscated or misaligned by implementing fabricated commitments • Roles and identities of new/existing executives remain unaltered or established actors can subvert and resist change	Established executives; existing units in the formal structure Chief Information Officer (CIO) (*MilanModa1*) Press Officer (*MilanModa1*) Director Credit and Treasury (*MilanModa2*) Retail Intelligence Manager (*MilanModa2*) Head Retail and Promotions (*MilanModa2*) Head Global Supply-Chain (*BritModa*)

[a]The names of fashion companies featured in this table (*MilanModa1*, *MilanModa2*, *MilanModa3*, *BritModa*, and *Maison Française*), whose executives have been interviewed and referenced in this book, are pseudonyms. Details of these fashion companies, branded websites, and projects are deliberately vague to disguise identities

The converse process, re-artification, results from a continuing support for maintaining gaps between formal organizational structure and work practice, even when institutional forces call for abandoning the approach (Table 3.1). Across cultural industries, re-artification materializes as a dogged pursuit by executives in the formal structure to continue regarding the nature of their work as unchangeable, even in the face of developments that suggest contrary indications (Shapiro and Heinich 2012). As pointed out, one way in which re-artification has recently resurfaced is the change in the written discourse of journalists in the fashion industry, who have set out to re-intellectualize fashion as a "subtle disavowal of commerce" (Van de Peer 2014, p. 456). From a neo-institutional perspective, re-artification occurs when new organizational units (such as, e-commerce) are being introduced in the formal organizational structure of fashion companies, but executives continue isolating them from the actual work practices associated with the work of these new units. The next sections will document these responses to organizational change.

Shifting Paradigms in the Fashion Industry

From 1970s to 1990s

As Bourdieu and Delsaut (1975, p. 22) have argued, the field of fashion is "situated at an intermediary position between the artistic field and the economic field". The gap between formal structure and material practice in fashion companies is epitomized by the reliance of fashion organizations on Bourdieu's intermediary brokers of taste (Bourdieu 1993a). In the fashion field, these intermediaries have traditionally been associated with the marketing power of fashion publications, such as *Vogue*, and the commercial power of large brick-and-mortar retailers, such as *Neiman Marcus, Saks,* and *Bloomingdales* in the US; *la Rinascente* in Italy; and *Harrods* in the UK. Large retailers, in particular, have maintained relationships with luxury fashion brands that are historically driven by explicit commercial considerations. Retailers can contribute as much as 80–95%[1] of the annual income in fashion companies. The commercial advantage of large merchants has resulted in extreme concentrations of power vis-à-vis fashion companies, and this has, obviously, affected how intensely fashion companies credit these partners with legitimacy advantages. The origins of the allegiance of fashion companies on merchant gatekeepers can be traced to the 1960s, when the industry swung into de-artification. French couturiers were supplanted by designer-créateurs, who set more reliably distinguishable styles with broader commercial appeal for large retailers (Crane 1997). The Director of *Fondazione Altagamma*—the Italian luxury brand committee representing the interests of Italian luxury fashion companies since 1992—explained the change:

> When I started working in this area in 1966 – 99.99 per cent of the products were channelized in the multi-brand stores.[2] Hardly any fashion brands at the time actually owned single-branded stores. Particularly, these were jewelry stores, *Bulgari, Cartier, Tiffany, Graaf, Asprey,* etc. But, not so many! And, the other end of the industry was leather bags, *Louis Vuitton, Salvatore Ferragamo, Gucci, Prada,* and *Coach.* But, apart from that, the majority of the goods were channelized through the multi-brands [i.e., large retailers].

The institutional system supporting these complex commercial and aesthetic relations between "key designers, magazine publications and shops" has remained decidedly hierarchical (Entwistle and Rocamora 2006, p. 738). As per one retail industry executive working at a global luxury retail consultancy in NYC, commercial relationships between fashion companies and large intermediaries, in fact, "have become so consolidated today that analyzing cultural trends in the few department stores that are left is not appealing anymore". The ongoing commercial consolidation of large retailers has also provided a basis for de-artification in the high-end of the fashion industry, because retailers have rendered the commercial aspects of fashion houses apparent over time. To be sure, fashion company executives have pushed against this development. "Retailers", the CIO of *MilanModa1* argued, "can issue a purchase order (PO) to a fashion brand, say, Gucci, yet the latter has the responsibility to do *all the rest*; specify the product, acquire the materials, get it from source, to a central distribution source, and eventually to Saks's premises".

Technology changes are another classic example of pushback to artification. The adoption of Electronic Data Interchange (EDI) technologies by fashion retailers have allowed US-based merchants to optimize their production streams, attaining the technical ability to request frequent changes in size and design for apparel contracted from high-fashion brands (Laudon and Traver 2013).[3] Executives in fashion companies with operational responsibility in production and distribution argued that these changes moved fashion company *créateurs* away from enjoying full autonomy in developing a collection.

> They [retailers] decided that they needed to have single standard format in order to receive information from all the different [fashion] brands, and essentially for each brand to use this technology. In reality, and this is true for most of the other fashion brands, EDI is just a service to the main clients, Neiman Marcus and Saks, *in order to be able to work with them.* This model works well when you sell T-shirts, but doesn't work when you sell high-fashion product. Our products have a very short life... Usually, they are born and die in one season. (CIO, *MilanModa1*)

In the 1980s, in an uncharacteristic move for the Italian fashion system, which is broadly characterized by raging rivalries between high-fashion brands (Mora 2006), Italian fashion companies formed a united front to what they perceived to be de-artification processes started by retailers. The Director at *Fondazione Altagamma* characterized this united move as a serious push toward re-artification in the industry:

> They pushed a lot – particularly, Italian companies, for the creation of *single-branded* stores; and they started opening their own single-branded stores, particularly in the US. And, when the department stores reacted, Versace, Armani, Zegna, and Gucci proposed to US department stores to open single-branded boutiques *within* their space.

As an institutionalized realm, the fashion industry is assembled around the themes of seasonality and trending. One of the reasons for frequent "trending" is the small-scale production by fashion companies, especially Italian and French fashion houses. A luxury fashion company locates its production in the country of origin, where control over smaller suppliers and quality checks of production samples are easier to perform. Small-scale production is necessary to control for ambiguities in the demand of large retailers, but this ambiguity makes it difficult for fashion companies to sustain and increase their revenue streams. This situation is made problematic also because large retail buyers want to have a say on design when PO leave for overseas production facilities. Ultimately, even after the fashion industry was reorganized from an artisanal affair to a vertically integrated organization (such as *Polo Ralph Lauren*), producing high-fashion garments continues to be a labor-intensive process. The Chief Information Officer (CIO) at *MilanModal* spelled out the problem of aligning production and retail demand:

> Technically, we have a very limited, very high-quality production and we don't want to be too pushy to our production facilities because they are not capable to see what really the production needs to be. In our example, we are talking about 100,000 SKUs a year, so it is not a lot. So, we are able to control very, very well the production, [in which] all these processes, from the first idea to the first sample, are done most of the time, manually.

A prominent example of boundary work where we can directly observe fashion organizations to legitimate the industry as an art form is evident in the "ceremony of consecration" (Entwistle and Rocamora 2006, p. 735) that plays out in the fashion field during seasonal Fashion Weeks. Fashion Weeks materialize the idea of decoupling between commercial obligations to retailers from the intellectual character of the runway practice of fashion companies (Kawamura 2004; Geczky and Karaminas 2012). Since the 1970s, high-fashion companies have engaged in a collective production of 'original design' practice by relying on peculiarly subversive techniques for communicating trends (Crane 1997). Through the late 1970s to mid-1990s, trends were communicated *directly, and exclusively to fashion industry insiders.* This systemic emphasis on artistic legitimation through selective communication of trends to insiders originates in the 1800s, when catwalk spectaculars, called "fashion parades" (Evans 2014) took place in Paris couture salons. Fashion parades were available exclusively for sellers and buyers and customers did not have access to them.

Fashion company brands were, furthermore, extremely reliant on original design, and "original design" was communicated at the seasonal fashion shows. The insider fashion community waited for the runways to see future trends. Endorsed by the industry's two powerful intermediaries, retailers and fashion press, trending was produced by only a few designers in the industry, considered to be creators of "original" trends. The original trendsetter of that decade, charged with the symbolic status of creating 'original' trends, was the Japanese house of Kenzo, headed by Kenzo Takada. The House of Kenzo had dramatic impact on the legitimation of derivative styles for the high-fashion industry, in part, due to Kenzo's symbolic capability to produce "a look that was so *definitive* each season that everyone in the industry could copy and did copy" (Creative Director, global fashion trend company, NYC, 2012). Photographers were not allowed at the seasonal shows, and attending trend experts learned to scribble quick illustrations of designs. Once produced, these illustrations were slid "under the doors of designers that did not have the opportunity to attend the show. *This is how trending was communicated*" (ibid., 2012).

Today, this pronounced 'isomorphic' approach to ritual legitimation of normatively acceptable fashion design has receded as an artifact of cultural importance in the fashion industry. As the industry continued chasing trends, as one industry pundit in global trending put it, "a lock-in effect for decades continued to feed the fashion industry only one lesson - the lesson of retro trending".

From 2008 to 2014

During the first ten years of this century—and particularly with the arrival of the global financial crisis in 2008—the artistic role of the fashion show has become somewhat obscured. This development is not new. As a field of practice, the fashion industry originated in seventeenth-century France in the court of Louis XIV and was instituted as a center of extremely lucrative commodity business. The mass commodification of the industry was, however, reinforced in 1943, when Eleanor Lambert founded the first commercial press event of its kind under the auspices of 'Press Week' in New York City. The institutionalization of Fashion Week contributed to exposing the commercial function of the fashion industry. In 2006, Entwistle and Rocamora observed during their study of London Fashion Week in the 2000s that, "while the distinction between art and commerce is translated into the planning of the space discussed above, the commercial dimension of fashion is not hidden, that is, it is not totally disavowed" (2006, p. 739).

The paradox was that while in the 1970s the artistic practices used to communicate reliable trends were newly minted, seasonal fashion shows today are forums where retro trending is communicated. The CEO at a global fashion trend company in NYC summarized this change in paradigm:

There was actually a time when trends were new. Fashion shows are *enter-tainment* today. They are creating brand awareness. Examples in the past five years have been two of the most stylistic shows. Alexander McQueen's in 2010 – dwelling on the theme of prehistoric birds, and Karl Lagerfeld's in Paris – based on a peasant girl fantasy of Marie Antoinette. From the runways, we don't even laugh at these unwearable creations.

A part of this devolution of status stems from the fact that consumers are well aware today that seasonal fashion shows carry an explicit commercial intent. "One of the things that have changed the paradigm", the Head of Retail and Promotions at *MilanModa2* noted, "is that customers now have access to these stupid fashion shows! In the past, the consumer didn't see 'the who', *only the trade side saw it*, and the trade people understood what to ignore and what to put their faith in." The Retail Intelligence Manager at *MilanModa2* similarly bemoaned, "How confusing is that? We are supposed to be the authorities! Designers are realizing that there is a problem with endless fashion shows".

Fashion Weeks coincide with the commercial high point in the year, when new collection samples are shown backstage to buyers as an occasion for gauging next season's bottom line with these clients. The eyes of outsiders are now accustomed to the visibility of commercial negotiations taking place during seasonal fashion weeks between fashion companies and retailers. Product samples presented by fashion labels to their clients differ substantially from samples displayed on the runway. Some fashion company practitioners—as the Head of Global Communications at *MilanModa3*—openly muse about the increased scrutiny that consumers have over this myth. "You know how it works", she noted. "Backstage with McQueen, the merchandise available for purchase and the styles available at retailers like Saks are not remotely the same thing. There is craziness on the stage, but the retailer walks into the fashion room and there is an entirely different range of sellable clothes." Post-runway negotiations with retailers are strategic commercial importance for fashion executives. "After we present our collection to the customer during fashion shows", noted the CIO at *MilanModa1*, "and once they select the product, we quickly place customer order in the system. And, immediately after we have customer orders, production needs to start a.s.a.p. to begin production."

Another important development that added fuel to the shifting imperatives of trending in the fashion industry was that between 2008 and

2010 fashion companies were publicly revealing their commercial vulnerability to the creditworthiness of their retailer partners. The solvency of retailers placed fashion brands at imminent financial peril. The VP of a large retail consulting firm in New York pointed out in 2010 that this systemic direction was inevitable, because Neiman Marcus and Saks had the advantage to be "too big to fail [...] for example, Macy's and J.C. Penney are bigger than most of the brands that they have".

In the worst period between 2008 and 2010, the Credit and Treasury Director at the NYC headquarters of *MilanModa2*, with operating revenue of €1.4 billion for 2010, had to wait up to 90 days to receive merchandise payments from Neiman Marcus and its largest store—Saks 5th Avenue. Both of these clients had accumulated "bad credits" and the brand had difficulty negotiating financing with the factor firm— the financial firm that typically backs credit lines for fashion companies until they receive account payables by retailers at the end of each season. However, the key systemic challenge faced by fashion companies was that contrary to the institutional logic of the industry during the latter part of the twentieth century, their Design teams now had to think how to produce designs that were increasingly *divergent* from designs by other luxury fashion companies. The Credit and Treasury Director of *MilanModa2* explained the changing paradigm:

> During the recession it was tough, because the factor could also go down. For a while, we did not have a factor. As of April 1 (2010), we have a new factor. Our factor company was able to reduce our surcharges because the risk was lower. In 2009, during the *recession the aim was to create products that the customer is buying.* And, for example, for March 2010, our retail sales were 1.6 per cent higher.

During the worst years of the financial crisis, in an attempt to raise consumer spending of ready-to-wear fashion, hungered for revenue CEOs at the largest US retailers increasingly contemplated overhauling their buying and distribution practice. As the tale of luxury shifted from the traditional association with "craftsmanship, timelessness, and heritage[4]" to luxury by "value" (not necessarily defined by high price), large retailers restructured their brand portfolios and advanced a new buying rhetoric to fashion company partners. The reinvented rhetoric proposed that (having satiated the consumer with high-price, high-fashion brands) the large department stores should now be getting luxury of a different kind.

The CEO of one of the largest brick-and-mortar fashion retailers presented this rationale for conceptual de-artification of trends to an audience of high-fashion companies:

> The four components: the product itself, the selling environment, the selling, and cost structure. Every one of them needs to be redefined. If you look at product – it's about value now. Customers want luxury products, but luxury products are differentiated, they're exclusive, they have limited distribution; they're not widely available, and that's what makes luxury special. But people want value. And value doesn't necessarily mean price. It could be price, but it's about quality, design; it's feeling that whatever they're buying, it is worth it.

The CEO of another large US retailer suggested to a comparable audience of high-fashion executives that they undertake similar approach to differentiation in design. The concept of "differentiated luxury" was eventually advanced by the fashion retail industry. Differentiated luxury meant that even when their apparel product was placed at differentiated (lower) price points, "a whole platter of brands that didn't exist a year ago" could still be classified as luxury, and "that's really the future" (CEO, US fashion retailer). Although some executives, such as the Head of Global Supply-Chain at *BritModa*, were certain that "the crisis will help to draw a defining line between luxury and fashion," other fashion pundits, as the Managing Partner of a global retail consultancy, submitted that "luxury became overused, overdesigned concept" that necessitated a new phase in the development of the fashion industry. The CEO of a large US fashion retailer simplified the request from industry's largest partners:

> In the *new world*, you've seen changes. I hope that we can focus on differentiation, 25-30 per cent products you can't find anywhere else. We need something, that they [customers] can't get anywhere else. Doesn't mean *brands* necessarily, but *products* you can't find anywhere else. *You're seeing a bifurcation – we talk about luxury – and luxury is at multiple price points.*

Accordingly, the ritualized practice where fashion companies collectively followed a trend leader became delegitimized and, in the eyes of outsiders, fashion shows appeared as de-artified occasions for negotiating next season's commercial bottom line with retailers. This redirection in priorities disrupted the highly institutionalized routines, on which high-fashion brands had built their commitments to retailers. An executive at a large US retailer suggested that brick-and-mortar fashion merchants rapidly began categorizing fashion companies as engaging in legitimate behavior only when design priorities in the latter reflected a *"hard commitment to quantities and soft commitment to clothing lines"*. At the same time as retailers cautioned couturiers that their adherence to designing after "artist geniuses" (Crane 2012, p. 138) could make their mutual commercial relationship problematic, design and creative executives across fashion companies were struggling to increase the "immaterial value" (Mora 2006, p. 348) of their product, dismissing narratives around the idea that fashion design has a commercial dimension. A senior designer in a US luxury fashion company, for example, argued that their creative team could not transition to designing lower-priced apparel, because "the nature of our designs is very unique [...] and we are a design-driven company". At *MilanModa2*, executives representing brick-and-mortar retail operations, employed similar rhetoric by reproving retailers of pushing to "create products that the customer *is* buying" (Retail Intelligence Manager, *MilanModa2*) and commercializing the industry by making "more money in chargebacks than in clothes" (Director Credit and Treasury, *MilanModa2*).

This period also witnessed continuing "negotiation of meaning at different levels of the [fashion] organization" (Mora 2006, p. 334), leading to further transformations in fashion companies. A problem of balance eventually emerged between creative teams and commercial planners, even in fashion companies considered to be among the most design-driven. This trend is best explained as another shift in behavior in fashion companies pursuant to emerging legitimacy concerns regarding what is considered to be acceptable design to retailers. The increasing complexity of forecasting and planning in fashion companies had permitted financial roles and functions, such as planning and merchandising, to become influential in *defining* seasonal collection. The kinds of questions that planners could influence were absolutely essential to the final collection, because not only quantities, but also *styles* were, in part, defined by these functions. Supply-chain experts corroborated that financial planning, not design, was taking the head position in fashion brands. "What usually happens", one Senior Analyst at a global consulting retail firm concluded, is that a new season starts in fashion with financial planning. They first start with the merchandising plan, then assortment planning, promotions, that is the seasonality of the items. All this is driven by a demand forecast [...] driving the allocation based on the forecast. At the end of the season, how do I clear that merchandise, which is seasonal in nature, and I don't want to carry, and how do I get the highest margin I can? Then they make a budget and within that budget they say: 'now, what assortment do I need to have to help me reach that financial goal?' Now they're starting to look at colors, types, and fabrics. They use historical sales information and forecasting to help them see where the market is moving in advance of what's going to be hot.

Design and trending pundits in the industry criticized that this latest development had further erased the necessary gap between aesthetics and commerce in fashion companies. A Creative Editor with the *Wall Street Journal* exclaimed at a retail meeting in 2010 that "major merchandising decisions now take place at a level that is *so far* removed from the selling floor...that the tail is wagging the dog." One of the principal designers at a US fashion company attested to this renegotiation of meaning:

> In fashion companies, design has always been completely free in every decision. Lately, it's a little bit like that – merchandise telling design what they can do; how big the line can be; how many new models they can design; in how many colors they can do the line, because it is based on how much they can sell. It's still a little bit of a bad situation, since when the line designer can't do what he wants, he goes straight to the Head Designer, and says, 'the merchandiser doesn't want me to edit new order, but I think you should press them'. And, obviously Head Designer says, go for it, but... It's been a constant back and forth.

ADAPTATION RESPONSES TO E-COMMERCE: FROM 'RE-ARTIFICATION' TO 'RESISTANCE TO ARTIFICATION'

In European high-fashion companies, conformity to institutionalized rules has resulted in a separation of roles and priorities within the formal organizational structure, with brick-and-mortar retail separated divisionally from communications. Roles and functions associated with communications in fashion companies are frequently the unit or division responsible for the production of 'artification' rhetoric. Communications divisions remain in charge of fashion companies' communication and presentation tools, negotiations with fashion publishers, and presentation of a "coordinated image" (Mora 2006, p. 346) to agents and retailers in their specific market. Retail divisions, on the other hand, are liable for making sure that the commercial terms and rhetoric with retailers are appropriately delineated.

The result is that even though a significant part of material practice in fashion companies includes activities that are explicitly commercial and are recognized as such, their ultimate interpretation is set by communications executives, who rule frequently in favor of aesthetic enterprise (Table 3.2). For example, promotion and marketing events were conceptualized by retail executives with strategic and procedural influence as "one of the most important generators of business" (Head of Retail and Promotions, *MilanModa2*), but as communications tools with a generic appeal to "love and buy our bloody pink shoes" (Head of Global Communications, *MilanModa3*). Customer relationship management (CRM), direct mail, and creative partnerships were similarly considered to be among the "most important aesthetic practice[s] in the lifetime of a fashion company", as per the Director of Digital Marketing at *Maison Française*. In short, even when these material practices were subordinated to the economic constraints of Retail divisions, their interpretation was being "invested with a truly cultural legitimacy" (Bourdieu 1993b, p. 112).

Table 3.2 The appeal of ceremonial/artified practice, 2010–2012

Practice	Content	Aesthetics/Commerce	Field
1. Events	Fashion shows	A	O
2. Direct mail	Cocktails	E	F
3. Partnerships	Notable guests	S	F
4. CRM	Style presentations	T	L
	Special new and limited editions	H	I
	promotions	E	N
	Gifts, sweepstakes, raffles	T	E
		I	
		C	
		S	
5. E-mail		COMMERCE	ONLINE

Source *MilanModa2*, adapted from internal reports, 2010–2012

The challenge for fashion companies in the coming digital era was to reframe their work repertoires and rhetoric associated with these, such that the introduction of e-commerce as both a commercial and an aesthetic practice would not be hijacked by either aesthetic or commercial rhetoric. This goal was challenged by the existing organizational structure in high-fashion companies, even in the rare cases where executives from established siloes prompted the changes.

One particularly striking example of pushback is *MilanModa2*—one of the largest global high-fashion brands whose revenue for 2016 reached €2.9 billion. The former Head of Retail and Promotions, currently Manager of Marketing and Events, reported that his intent to "push digital" was not well taken by senior executives at headquarters in Milan. His rationale for expanding the mix of practice developed by Communications (Table 3.2) to the online channel, was that even though "80 per cent of the business is driven by 20 per cent of the customers, it's important to get the other 80 per cent of customer base shopping. The internet gives us a broad reach opportunity". The company's PR Department, which reported to Communications, moved to open a Facebook page in 2010 and ruled that until further notice, this was going be the only push for any Internet practice, associated with marketing and aesthetics. The Head of Retail and Promotions eventually shifted his responsibilities by assuming a transversal role and liaising directly with Communications and Retail to broaden the type of activities associated with e-commerce.

A more frequent organizational response in the industry has been that of *MilanModa1* and *MilanModa3*. In *MilanModa3*, an iconic Milanese brand, whose revenue for 2012 was a little over €2 billion, two new but separate units were founded in 2012 to jumpstart the practice of e-commerce. The first unit, termed *Social Media*, was placed under the Communications division. The second unit, *e-commerce*, was separated structurally and placed under the existing Retail division (Fig. 3.1). This organizational setup ensured that the existing divisions between aesthetic and commercial work repertoires would be carried over to the new e-commerce practice, and that e-commerce executives would have to traverse two diverging rhetorical frames to manage a single integrated practice.

As in *MilanModa1*, the new Head of Global Digital Marketing at *MilanModa3* requested symbolic autonomy from Communications emphasizing the importance of combining commercial and aesthetic

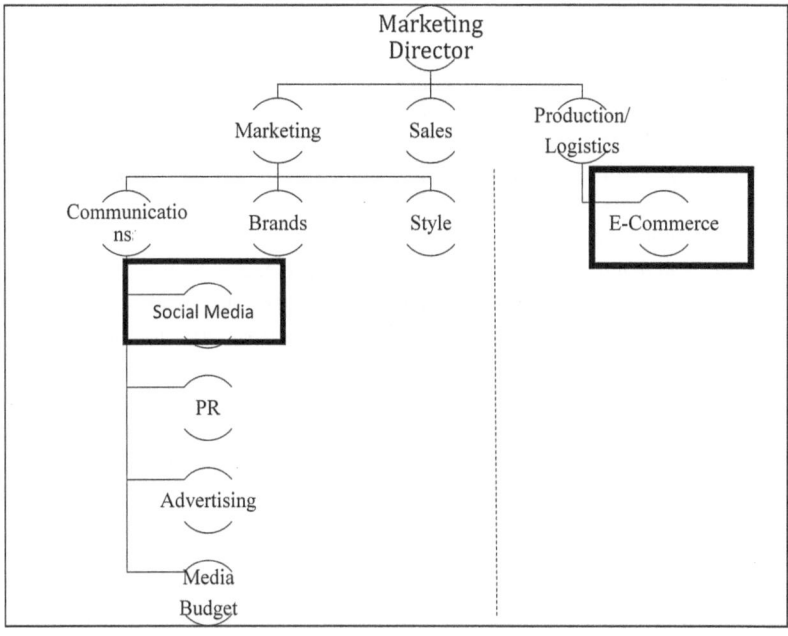

Fig. 3.1 Organizational structure at *MilanModa3* (*Source* Adapted from interviews. Simplified organizational structure)

practice when developing the content of e-commerce campaigns specific to the online channel. He noted that in e-commerce, everyday practice revolved around combining commercial and aesthetic outcomes:

> We need key performance indicators (KPI) even for Social Media. It is always changing but we want to define some KPIs, like number of fans; number of interactions; number of comments; number of likes; number of shares. Because it is easy to have 1 million fans on Facebook! You just buy ad space and say, come here and you have 1 pair of free jeans. But, you know... [pause] this is not what we need; we need engagement *and* sales.

This persuasion was unsuccessful. Keeping new units siloed within existing brick-and-mortar divisions permitted executives with strategic influence in Communications and Retail to maintain separation between formal structure and material practice and exert control over the newly proposed, and thus, culturally foreign practices. Whereas in *MilanModa3* e-commerce was placed under the commercially driven Retail division, in *Maison Française*, the pendulum swung in the other direction and e-commerce was placed under the total patronage of Global Communications. The Director of Digital Marketing at *Maison Française* problematized the organizational placement as a "*cultural prohibition*" in which the "Global Communications Division *misinterprets the meaning* of the Internet, which has grown out of the communications stage and into the collaborative stage." This organizational configuration allowed Communications to exert strategic oversight over the production of new practice, thereby extending the regulatory reach of organizational structure already associated with favoring artification rhetoric (Fig. 3.2).

The Director of Digital Marketing in *Maison Française* explained the brewing conflict between his team and Communications executives as a symbolic misalignment between directives set forth by the formal structure and actual work repertoires:

> One person for E-Commerce on the Internet and one guy for Communications on the Internet – it is not possible. In fact, in fashion companies, they *don't know* where to put us - the people of the Internet. Because, it's E-Commerce, but it's also bloggers - it's public relations. In

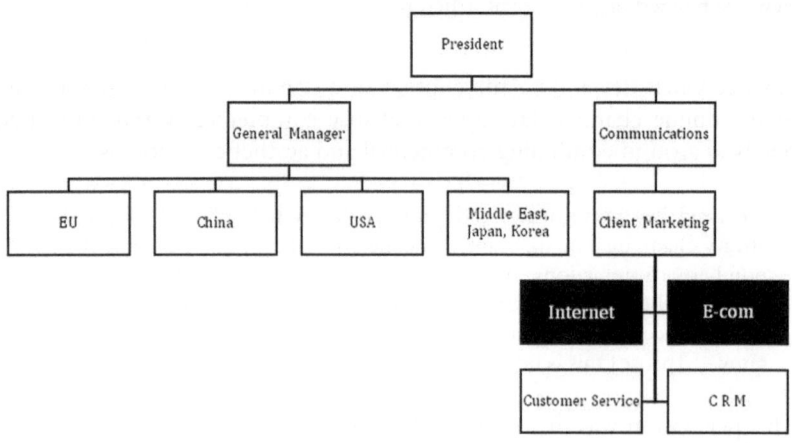

Fig. 3.2 Keeping Artification Afloat: Formal Organizational Structure at *Maison Française* (*Source* Adapted from interviews. Simplified organizational structure)

France, Europe, they always put us either in Retail or in Communications and it never works. For this to work, you have the e-Communications, marketing, all at the same level [for the] Internet.

The conclusion was clear. New creative professionals in fashion companies required symbolic autonomy for the production of material practice in e-commerce, away from the existing institutionalized rhetoric of artification and sovereignty from sanctions imposed by Communications or Retail. The two in-depth case studies presented below stand out among the most intriguing and diverging responses observed in luxury fashion companies in the period.

RE-ARTIFICATION: MAINTAINING THE GAP BETWEEN STRUCTURE AND PRACTICE

MilanModal is a high-fashion Italian label established in 1970s that is structurally similar to the privately owned Prada and the public Gucci, with around €340.2 million revenue in 2011. The company was among the many fashion brands with tremendous operating losses between 2008–2011, necessitating heavy restructuring for cost saving. The e-commerce 'Home Design' experiment at *MilanModal* is a unique example of re-artification and institutional resistance to supporting e-commerce practice in the fashion industry. The approach of executives with strategic influence in *MilanModal* was to formally introduce their engagement with developing and testing an e-commerce website, but obfuscate the lack of actual e-commerce capability on said website and any work repertoires in e-commerce by channeling a rhetoric of artification.

The organizational structure at *MilanModal* was a mix between *Maison Française* and *MilanModa3*. The e-commerce unit was placed under the Retail division, with acknowledgement from Retail executives that its function was tied to commercial logic. However, another team, termed 'Internet', was founded and placed under Communications. These organizing moves preserved the gap between formal organizational structure and work practice and made it difficult for executives in either new unit to coordinate work repertoires across e-commerce. The actual work of the 'Internet' team in *MilanModal* comprised of press officers who developed social media content approved by the Communications division. Accordingly, the perception of executives from established divisions was that the daily work repertoires of the Internet team was sanctioned by Global Communications in order to "*control* Communications outside of our company" (CIO, *MilanModa1*) and therefore, enforce a rhetoric associated with aesthetics. Valid as this perception may have been, Global Communications exercised this unusual control only with regard to the new in-house Internet team. As pointed out by the CIO at *MilanModa1*, this was not an incidental move. The Communications division commonly outsourced the production of press releases for social media to external agencies. "It is a company in NYC", the CIO pointed out, "but I forgot the name. We have a partnership with them. They *propose* what to publish. They are not *completely* independent." Nonetheless, online content produced in-house was controlled "at all costs in *all* brand-related content" (CIO, *MilanModa1*). This unusual openness of Communications executives in allowing external parties to handle the production of some press content, but deny similar room for maneuver to in-house digital executives, suggests that the goal of these strategic executives was to assimilate new structures and practices along established and rationalized institutional lines.

Initiation to digital practice at *MilanModa1* started with a decision by the Creative Director and the CIO to redesign the company's corporate website and offer visitors and prospective customers browsing capability and video of runway collections. The revamping of the corporate website in 2010 was a first step in the direction to initiating e-commerce. The CIO heading the feasibility team, contended that in reorganizing for the Internet, the company should continue exerting strategic influence over the content of any new practice by outsourcing "all the logistics function to somebody else, and keep all marketing in-house. Once we have control of marketing", noted the CIO, "and have control of the look and feel, we don't have a problem to allow our distribution service to somebody else."

The idea to outsource functions related to the logistics side of e-commerce was an unstated agreement by company executives to duplicate their existing relationships with brick-and-mortar retailers online. There were three scenarios for fashion companies to go about building e-commerce: in-house, by collaborating with *Digital Moda*, or have the web design completed by a smaller digital agency. *MilanModa1* was opting to eventually develop e-commerce internally, but relinquish the logistics to an outside party that owned and operated distribution facilities.

This decision required *MilanModal* to sell their actual fashion inventory in bulk ahead of expected online sales, to another company, similar to *Digital Moda*, which would then manage what fashion product to put on *MilanModal*'s e-commerce website and distribute product sold to consumers.

Strategic executives, as *MilanModal*'s CIO, were accustomed to selling apparel to merchants, like Neiman Marcus, in bulk. When shop-within-shop was first introduced as a concept in brick-and-mortar retail, large merchants acquired the product of fashion houses in return for autonomy in deciding on how to curate their own shop floors. Selling fashion apparel in bulk to e-commerce fashion retailers, however, was equal to *relinquishing* control over the same function: *curation* of fashion product online. In short, with "insider" partners, the actual commercial aspect of the relationship could successfully be kept separate from the ascribed aesthetic sentiment. With "outsider" brokers of taste, however, the same institutional logic was missing from the equation and identical practices were seen as attempts at de-artification. The CIO explained the reasoning:

> If we do sell them the product, they get to decide which product they want to put on the site. In the end, they *compromise* the image. Even if they are doing the website like we want it, *even if we have complete control* over the way the website is executed, [...] at the end, they are in charge to speak to the customer, they are in charge to propose the product, to collect the money.

One of the significant problems of handling a transition online for the CIO and the Creative Director was to retain control of communications in partnering with an e-commerce provider. In 2009, *MilanModal* started negotiations with *Digital Moda* executives in order to probe building of an e-commerce capability. In early 2010, the CIO was cautiously optimistic about possible partnership, if *Digital Moda* were to keep away from managing any of the brand's marketing online. "We will outsource all the logistics function to somebody else", he held, "and keep all marketing in-house. In this way, we can keep the image and the size, but do not make any big investments".

In mid-2010, the CIO was in preliminary negotiations with *Digital Moda* on assessing options for developing e-commerce. In its potential role as a co-creator of *MilanModal*'s e-commerce identity, *Digital Moda* required as per standard contract to have a say and a share of revenue in designing and managing parts of e-commerce related to marketing campaigns for fashion brands. The standard clause was to manage a fashion brand's search engine optimization (SEO[5]) program. This meant to optimize the e-commerce property for search to help bring in traffic, convert potential browsers into shoppers, and generate sales and revenue. *MilanModa1* executives demurred. Any future partnership with *Digital Moda* was to be kept at the most basic level of a technology provider. Held the CIO:

> Once we have control of marketing, and have control of the look and feel, we don't have a problem to allow our *distribution service* to somebody else. The reality is that until 3 years ago, nobody had this capability in-house, so that's why nobody was doing this. [*Digital Moda*] just in two years developed this capability and is able to offer it to the brands. And most of the brands don't have the internal investment; but, we would like to use [*Digital Moda*] to do the job and we do all the marketing.

The CIO was at a cultural crossroads. He understood that a partnership with *Digital Moda* would require the brand to sign a contract, accepting someone else's take on how to practice on the new channel. The executive reasoned as to why *Digital Moda* could be the "right" partner. It seemed that moral and pragmatic legitimacy was not the problem. "They are very good. They do everything", noted the CIO. "They design the website; they are in charge of the fulfillment and customer service. In some cases, they also own the inventory and in others, we own it. Very good marketing ideas, but!" Instead, the worry centered on retaining *MilanModa1*'s "original" cultural identity, as the CIO understood it:

> But... *we don't want to give our brand image in the hands of someone else.* Even if they are doing the website like we want it, *even if we have complete control* over the way the website is executed, at this stage we are not feeling confident to give our image to someone else. In the end, they are in charge to speak to the customer, they are in charge to propose the product, to collect the money and at the end we get some partial commission... Depends which completeness of the process *they want to own.*

In the end, it came to an impasse. If *MilanModa1* agreed to dispose of inventory risk by selling its fashion product in bulk to *Digital Moda* (which in turn agreed on creating marketing strategies to curate and sell this inventory), *MilanModal* could lose creative control over the product curated online. "If inventory risk is in our hands", the CIO said, "We can have leverage. If inventory risk is in their hands, they get to decide. If we do sell them the product, they get to decide which product they want to put on the site. In the end, they *compromise* the image." The CIO was a cautious change agent. He assumed that the established behavior of the company in the brick-and-mortar domain was the only appropriate identity for *MilanModal*. The CIO summed up these conflicting prerogatives as a tug-of-war between aesthetics and commerce:

> If we sell it to you, you can say: red dresses we do not want to buy, because red dresses do not sell well, but black dresses we will. So, in some way, they do compromise the image of the brand. The idea is to shift the attention from the product to the brand. You think about [*MilanModal*] first, and then, you approach the product. This of course, in some way, reduces the number of potential customers, but we want to go back to be an efficient company.

Even though, in late 2010, the CIO became was disinclined to talk about e-commerce as an internal project—"What I'm saying is", he stated, "we are not going to do this project internally, because the cost and the complexity of making an E-Commerce site is not convenient"—subsequently, he announced that talks were taking place on the options for experimenting with e-commerce internally. This internal project, called the 'Home Design' experiment, showcased the far reaches of ceremonial conduct in *MilanModal*. A feasibility team of reorganizing for the Internet was formalized in 2011 at *MilanModal*. The Creative Director (also, the CEO) and the CIO spearheaded the project. The perception of the feasibility team was that the less "culturally risky" e-commerce product to introduce was the line of apparel, branded as Home Design.[6] Visually, the redesigned corporate website of the company was optimized for discovery on the largest search engines and a link to the Home Design e-commerce page was added to the front page of the corporate website. Yet, the Home Design page did not have *actual shopping* capability put in place. Prospective customers could access the e-commerce link and browse fashion product related to the Home Design collection, but—contrary to the proclaimed goal of the e-commerce experiment—could not purchase merchandise online. The actual functional capability of e-commerce, ordering, back-end, and fulfillment, were missing and never developed. There was no awareness campaign to induce potential customers to discover the website, such as buying Google search keywords or placing banners on content-heavy online magazines. On the Home Design page, there was no registration offered to track the buying habits of the browsing few, who ended up finding this webpage. No email marketing campaigns were ever developed, before 2009 and well into 2010, as part of a structure of an emerging e-commerce unit. The communications team consistently avowed their confidence that "new" customers would, somehow, without the website being indexed on search engines, know exactly how to get to it. The "experiment" ran its course with executives aware at the extremely low odds for potential customers to discover the website.

Why did the CIO along with creative and communications teams, invest in e-commerce whatever, if the Home Design webpage had no e-commerce function? The CIO, architect of the redesign experience, argued that the main idea of this experiment was to *control the idea* of e-commerce, similarly to *MilanModal*'s approach in its own brick-and-mortar shops. The CIO explained that:

> When we open the store, our own store or via retailers [i.e., retailers like Neiman Marcus], we sign a contract that we do not allow anyone to open a similar store in a similar area in order to have full control of the distribution. At the moment that you allow an E-Commerce site to distribute all over the country, because you cannot control, if the product is in NYC or LA... We are extremely careful to move in this way. The only possibility could be to sell a *very different* product. In this way, you do not create distribution problems [...], in this way you preserve your own identity to the customer.

After the corporate website was redeveloped and more relevant searchable keyword content was introduced for easier pickup by search engines, more people began visiting it. The CIO reported that "we began to see some results *not really in terms of sales value*, but in traffic; how many people that are passing the website. We have about 500,000 unique visitors per month to access the main site. Visiting the Home Design are 45,000 people out of these unique visitors." The CIO dismissed the argument that increased traffic to the company's website would eventually lead to sales on the Home Design website, if the latter did include e-commerce capability. He did not integrate the concept of 'online traffic' as a culturally meaningful prerequisite to shopping. The term 'traffic' was relevant only to the assigned meaning it already had in the brick-and-mortar world: the entry and exit of people into a store. "Our product is very peculiar, either you like it or not", was the verdict. "You cannot just browse it like IKEA. [We have a] more specific type of customer with a specific taste."

Effectively, the new 'Internet' team had no decision-making power in the experiment. The new e-commerce team served a purely ceremonial function. The programmatic goal was to infuse any new work repertoires with the existing ritual practice at *MilanModal*. This assertion can be demonstrated by the desire of traditional executives to maintain the rhetoric of artification. The CIO at *MilanModal* unambiguously affirmed:

> It is something that was unsuccessful from the start, meaning that the website was not advertised. There was no online, direct marketing that announced the website to the world; positioning on the search engine, not much of it. We wanted to use the available tools in-house and see how the market out there reacts to the product. There wasn't much success, because the customer did not know anything about it.

Strategic executives deliberately sidestepped commercial exposure; precisely, what the introduction of e-commerce intended. The 'Internet' unit was effectively decoupled from day-to-day work repertoires anticipated in such divisions, such as search engine marketing (SEM),[7] banner advertising, or email campaigns that would have estimated the likelihood for commercial success of Home Design for company executives. The experiment, though not in any way associated with an experiment at all, ran its course with executives wholly aware at the extremely low odds for potential customers to discover or purchase the product. Formal structure and accepted rhetoric were decoupled from the content of actual e-commerce practice, in an attempt to 'reartify' the discourse as it became clear to *MilanModal* executives that to have an e-commerce website opened up questions of commercial intent within the existing organizational structure. The CIO, architect of the redesign experience, concluded that the goal of the trial was to indeed "*control the idea* of E-Commerce by controlling fully the experience and [...] capitalize on the image, not on the product."

In 2011, after formal conclusion of Home Design, company executives proceeded cautiously to a new approach to executing a future e-commerce experiment. The Communications division agreed to free funds for SEO in making the website "searchable" to browsing public, who were not regular customers of the brand. The feasibility team decided to invite a local media agency to work on SEO. The investment was small, and the fear of handling any e-commerce discussion as an opportunity was palpable. The CIO did not relent that to make future e-commerce highly searchable was not part of the "core" cultural apparatus of the company:

> It is not that important to be searchable. No, not that important. If somebody wants our product, they can go to the brand page immediately; *they don't have to think of anything else.* Until now we do not present products but we present image. You find the image, runway show, but you don't see anywhere the cost of the dress, etc. because we wanted to capitalize on the image not on the product.

In a compromise between 'thinking' and 'doing', *MilanModal* permitted the outside agency take charge in investigating the development of an e-commerce website, such as "the production, development, and shooting of product [for the website], etc., but *based totally on our directions*" (CIO). The minimum engagement was to have a Creative Director talking to another Creative Director from the media agency. Upon the negotiation of the look and feel for a future website, further roles would eventually be hired, such as copyrighters and web editors. "If we are lucky to get enough money for this", said the CIO, further expressing his apprehension, "there is somebody else besides the Creative Director, let's call them a copyrighter... this is a person who has full access to our content books and they pick the *right* information to put on the website, at the *right* moment, with the *right* content on the website." Even though this rhetoric suggested there was a transformation of culture toward accepting new practice, the persistence of a rhetoric of exclusivity and fear was evident in the multiple hedges against risk and sluggish procedure for the design of a future e-commerce website.

Over the next few years, the feasibility team at *MilanModal* continued signaling distress over losing any perceived control of the brand stemming from any promising collaboration with e-commerce fashion consultants, as *Digital Moda*. Executives at *MilanModal* associated e-commerce with a very high risk of brand recognition loss, stemming from their uncertainty on whether to accept new rhetoric and match it with new work practice. It is this fact that led administrators to further revert to thinking of placing e-commerce indefinitely under the Retail division in the future, and thereby dissociate the unit from any other function but fulfillment of customer orders. The CIO, nevertheless, understood the deficiencies of the approach:

> For the Italian shop, online retail is just another store. We never moved to the next level to think that the online store is something completely different. [pause] It is something broader; needs more [pause] more activities [pause] different activities, than a regular store. If you keep it under Retail, there is very clear ROI.[8] If you put it here, because Communications, really, it is very difficult to measure... Even if you were the best in the world, the results from the communications campaign would come in a few months. If you put the store under retail, the departments under retail have to present results every month; they are more immediate; they are measured on what they are doing now.

The CIO knew that the Communications division was not ready—in an epistemological sense—to agree to the development of e-commerce. A compromise that integrated marketing and sales activities somewhat was finally considered, and the CIO envisioned that in the future e-commerce unit, there would be a "dotted line between marketing [located under Communications] and the Retail division. If we grow more, I can imagine that in the future marketing will be added at the Retail division level to take care of E-Commerce." It would be another two years before *MilanModa1* opened a fully functioning e-commerce operation.

RESISTANCE AGAINST ARTIFICATION: CLOSING THE GAP BETWEEN STRUCTURE AND PRACTICE

When Shapiro and Heinich (2012) defined intermittent artification, they noted occasions when "resistance against artification" took place in cultural industries. Between 2010 and 2012, the Global Marketing Team at *BritModa* ran into this challenge upon discovering that peers in Europe—*MilanModa1, MilanModa2, MilanModa3*, and *Maison Francaise*—siloed their e-commerce units in-between Communications and Retail divisions. *BritModa* decided to organize in the opposite direction. One of the oldest fashion companies in the UK, *BritModa* represents a unique case of entrepreneurial moves in e-commerce, in that its internal e-commerce organization emulates that of e-commerce pioneers, like *Digital Moda*. The then-Vice President of Global Marketing was, in fact, an Internet enthusiast who diligently read *Internet Retailer*—as opposed to *Vogue*—and came up with an interesting vision for the company's e-commerce. Since 2009, an enthusiastic CEO, who had held a similar position for a very different US fashion brand, likewise joined in. The openness of this company to new cultural practice was facilitated by the openness of its executives—CEO, marketing and supply-chain— to discern broad advantages in other industries from adopting e-commerce. The Vice President of Global Marketing recounted the ideas that prompted him to suggest to his superiors the need to experiment with new "collaborative tools for brand positioning", as he was keen on explaining e-commerce. "I have the extraordinary opportunity to advance thinking in a new way", recounted the executive, offering thinking that was startlingly similar to *Digital Moda*'s founders, whose story we will start reading in Chapter 4. He continued:

> By this I mean the *maturing of the Internet* moving into web 2.0 about four years ago. ... *Before 2.0 in my opinion, the Internet was a communications and commerce platform.* And then, with the advent of Web 2.0 the desire to connect people, to develop a community behavior, what you moved towards was the development of an entertainment, interaction, and collaboration base. [...] Not all our peers were engaging in this behavior, so the opportunity was there for us to grab. As a result, when I started, I hired a lot of new people and replaced old people.

The VP of Global Marketing arrived from a consulting background and responded speedily to what he perceived was a need to adapt to new technologies for positioning of the company. Headquarters in London centrally drove core departments in *BritModa* such as Marketing, IT, and Supply-Chain, and their corollary decision-making depended on fundamental instructions from above. From this organizational configuration, executive management began the process of transitioning to "a sectoral [*sic*] system, corporately run and driven with essentially, a state". The success of e-commerce, the VP of Marketing thought, depended on hiring specialists with diverse backgrounds that had already served businesses known for their creativity in solving tech problems for creative companies outside of fashion. The executive underlined his approach in hiring people with legitimacy in e-commerce, *instead* of fashion:

I hired a guy from Xbox – on the marketing side, a guy from Nokia, a guy from an advertising agency. In the Media Department, I created a Digital Media side and hired a specialist in SEO. And, I spent time working with the PR team, make sure that they were engaging with digital. In conjunction to that, the rest of the system was changing, so I found great partners in the IT team. As I joined, there were also people across [*BritModa*] who were at that time trying to stimulate change.

Prior to the reorganization, *BritModa* was one of few fashion companies that had adopted e-commerce already in 2006. The surprising approach of executives was their agreement across the organizational structure to assess the value of e-commerce as a *commercial* opportunity. "A risky project with an exploratory dimension", recalled the Head of Global Supply-Chain—an established function with characteristically conservative approach to technology and practice. He then noted that ensuring buy-in in the company was a must:

> There was recognition within the company that E-Commerce was *part of the commercial future of the company*. The idea was to establish a presence, *learn from the behavior, and not wait* until you have the other brands collectively establish that E-Commerce is something you should engage in. 'Cause there is quite a movement towards collective collaboration in all sectors. Kind of follow the herd mentality. Brands gain confidence from other' brands behavior. But, this doesn't mean that the opportunity has been *positively explored*. It was seen as strategic commercial opportunity.

Executives in charge of building work repertoires associated with the new practice—the VPs of Global Marketing and Media Planning—budgeted the risk of failure for e-commerce to be "similar to the risk you encounter at a normal retail level". E-commerce and online marketing were first introduced as projects driven by existing supply-chain and Information Technology (IT) divisions, chaired by executives with strategic and procedural influence. Similarly, to what *MilanModal* eventually accomplished, executives in supply-chain and IT hired a consulting agency to build the e-commerce platform. However, as *BritModa* gained experience with e-commerce as a commercial pursuit in 2010, its executives developed interest in following the progress of new practices in Co-branding and curation, introduced by e-commerce fashion companies, like *Digital Moda*; which, itself became increasingly a point of comparison. The Vice President of Global Marketing—an executive with strategic and procedural influence—explained that e-commerce was evolving to be seen as an enabler of an integrated, "engagement and performance culture" in the company. In other words, the VP of Marketing was warming up to the idea of integrating among aesthetic and commercial goals.

The set of practices that followed comprised the approach of resistance to artification and narrowed the rhetorical gap between formal structure and actual work practice. The VP of Global Marketing understood that e-commerce required an integration approach, where actual work practice matched the rhetoric supported by the formal structure. Contrary to the idea expressed by *MilanModal*'s CIO that even without e-commerce, customers will flock to gawk at a website, just as they did in retail stores, and later make an appointment to visit a *MilanModal* retail store, the VP of Marketing at *BritModa* asserted that:

> [R]egardless of the general knowledge the consumer has for the brand offline, online it's a different game. It's fast paced and you have to garner new capabilities. It's the search engine that ranks you to the audiences who search, not your offline store, or your offline advertisement. So, instead of working with *Elle* or *Vogue* for making your audience aware of you, Google provides you with the platform and the rules for using it that are democratic. You also collaborate with search engine players on testing new technologies to better position the outcomes from a search with regard to the brand.

Thus, to recap, the approach of marketing executives in *BritModa* was to launch e-commerce with the expectation of overseeing a risky *commercial* project with an exploratory dimension. The Head of Global Supply-Chain explained that the accord to align existing rhetoric, produced by longstanding executives in the formal organizational structure with actual e-commerce work practice created by new executives, demonstrated the willingness to reshuffle roles and identities of actors across the company:

> Within the company, E-Commerce was part of the *commercial* future of the company. The idea across the company was to establish a presence, learn from the behavior, and finally, not wait until you have the other brands collectively establish that E-Commerce is something they should engage in. It was seen as *strategic commercial opportunity*.

The VP of Global Marketing upheld this approach in executive meetings. It "is not about embracing all technologies at all times", he hypothesized, "but about the use [of] the right medium in the right way." By early 2010, the transformation was complete. The e-commerce team was placed under Global Marketing, with existing Retail and Communications divisions only loosely related to e-commerce by way of supporting logistics. The e-commerce team secured its own marketing budget for advertising campaigns online, and got independence from Communications in planning and developing the content of communications campaigns.

Between 2010 and 2012, e-commerce merged with Digital Media—a new unit in charge of developing marketing and social media campaigns. The difference between *BritModa* and the other fashion studies in this book could not be overestimated. Whereas new e-commerce teams in *MilanModa3* and *MilanModa1* remained under the purview of Communications and became variously referred to as Social Media or Internet and were associated with work on public relations, in *BritModa*, e-commerce acquired independence in all areas, including typical campaigns in banner placement and not so typical Co-branding and curation. The final placement of e-commerce effectively separated the new unit from the institutionalized authority of Retail and Communications divisions. *BritModa* was moving away from ceremonial practice by aligning formal structure with the content of actual work repertoires in e-commerce.

Examples of this integration between commercial and aesthetic intent were shifts in thinking about the relationship between commerce and aesthetics introduced by executives in Global Marketing throughout the company following the introduction of e-commerce. The Director of Media, for example, posited that the behavior of *BritModa* customers online could be conceptualized as a practice of "symbolic purchasing". The average purchase value on the e-commerce website of *BritModa* lingered at around $200; less than 5 times the price of the brand's most popular apparel product. The Director of Media hypothesized—just as Bourdieu did in 1993—that customers were purchasing lower-cost items to experience the brand as a symbolic identifier of status. This was a prime example of integrating commercial with aesthetic goals in e-commerce, as part of a longer-term strategy to *"integrate E-Commerce into more marketing"* by the Head of Global Marketing.

Similarly, in 2012, the VP of Global Marketing re-conceptualized how the company evaluated success in e-commerce. The new idea was to look at the practice as a balancing act between "the *quality* and the *level* of [internet] traffic". Whereas the *level* of traffic was understood as a numeric expression of commercial intent, the *quality* of traffic was an aesthetic measure of intent, evaluated on the basis of social media content, posted by "fans" engaging in browsing *BritModa*'s e-commerce website and blog, to "experience the brand". The Director of Media underscored that the future value of the company depended on this integrated thinking:

> All marketing activity is creating something with a *commercial opportunity* for a brand, but it's not necessarily about *direct purchase*. There are very few examples of browsing behavior – especially from social media – that lead to purchase. The Internet is less about *telling* consumer things and more about *brand behaving* in a way, which is relevant to customers and the consumer making the decision on how to engage with the brand.

Consequently, *BritModa* was one of the first high-fashion companies where the role of the Director of Media shifted away from maintaining advertising relationships with fashion *magazines*—like Vogue—to building relationships with *online advertisers*, such as Google. The Director of Media continued to generate ideas on how to best explain this integration between aesthetic and commercial culture. Executives in Global Marketing agreed on the e-commerce slogan "engagement and performance culture", in which commercial and aesthetic goals were integrated. An example of this approach is the *beta* test offered by *Google* to *BritModa* during an advertising campaign in 2012. The Director of Media observed that the Global Marketing team could use an exclusively commercial tool—SEM—as a measure of brand engagement with the company's apparel product online. "We are now able to think about how we can use search to—of course it will still be mainly about driving revenue—buy keywords to make us money", he said. "But, also", smiled the executive,

> to start using search more intelligently, starting to use search more as a branding tool. In a funny way, we already do that. In certain markets, we don't make any money from our brand name. We always make sure that whenever someone types [our brand name] into a search engine that we

will appear at the top. And, we will do that even if we lose money doing that. So, you could argue in a really funny kind of way that that is actually branding. I mean, it's a long way from booking an ad in Vogue. But, it helps us to be able to display out product better.

BritModa aligned what it was 'saying' (i.e., the rhetoric associated with a practice) with what it was 'doing' (i.e., the content of actual practice). The result was that e-commerce executives reconsidered the value of existing practices espoused for a long time by the established organizational structure at *BritModa*. For example, the Global Marketing team resisted looking at banner advertising (a practice where a company buys space to display online ads or print editorials) as a product that carried an aesthetic value for the company. The established doctrine in Communications was that buying paper-based or online advertising space held aesthetic goals associated with brand influence. The Director of Media, however, opposed this traditional view. He noted that display advertising online should be driven by very different assumptions than those employed in print advertising with fashion magazines. When a fashion company paid Vogue to display a product, *BritModa* could gather very little demographic data that was useful for gauging the aesthetic or commercial result from such a campaign. The Director of Media considered that paper advertising was an outdated *"guessing game* that people seeing the ad are going to be right for the brand [...] or would respond to the brand".

As a departure from this 'guessing game' rhetoric, the goals of online advertising at *BritModa* were changing. The ability to track the exact number of unique visitors looking at a single banner or clicking on a banner prompted the Director of Media to commercialize the use of branded advertising away from aesthetics discourse and into commercial ground. This enactment of commercial logic to a practice executed previously only to reward existing institutional rules of conduct between fashion companies and their intermediaries, was unprecedented in equivalent fashion companies, without the training and learning provided by players, such as *Digital Moda*.

The VP of Global Marketing further conceptualized the work on integrating commercial and aesthetic rhetoric in using e-commerce tools as a "revenue-driven branding" whose goal was to resist any upcoming plans for re-artification, coming from the Communications division (Fig. 3.3). "In the same way that I've talked about using SEO to do more branding

Fig. 3.3 Moving between commerce and art: resistance against artification in digital practice

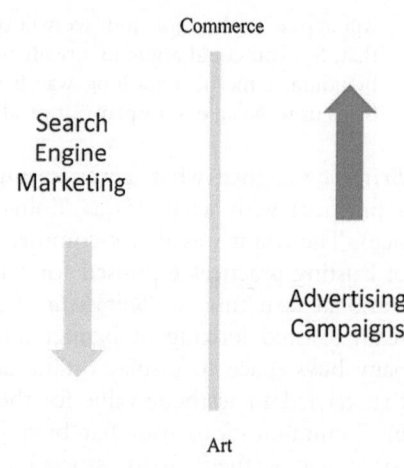

Commerce

Search
Engine
Marketing

Advertising
Campaigns

Art

and *art stuff*", he pointed out, "we are now looking at ways in which we can use our display assets to actually drive revenue for every dollar we make for this type of advertising, we make 7 dollars back". An example of revenue-driven branding was and continues to be the practice of "retargeting", used widely in e-commerce. Retargeting is an e-commerce tool that tracks the path of potential customers after they leave a website by continuing to place a visual ad in front of them; bouncing together with the customer as the customer continues to browse away. As we might surmise, retargeting was not popular in the fashion industry and was not used in *MilanModa1, MilanModa2*, or *Maison Française*, because of the implied weakening of aesthetic positioning of high-fashion companies. The logic of retargeting was commercial, but in *BritModa* the VP of Global Marketing theorized that retargeting had, in addition, aesthetic implications. "Rather than buying 50,000 impressions on Vogue.com—the online version of the fashion periodical," he noted "—we could actually buy the cookies of people who've been on the [E-Commerce] website. As they get on the Internet, we can effectively retarget them with advertising. This ad would have originally been designed as a branding piece for us; now we can use it to generate revenue as well".

NOTES

1. Internal company data, extrapolated from interviews with fashion companies, featured in this book.
2. Here "multi-brand" is used in the sense of shop-within-shop; a long-term the retail practice of large merchants to house individual fashion brands within assigned spaces on the premises of their retail locations.
3. The transactions involved transmitting a standardized message from one computer to another before the Internet. EDI now involves using the Internet for transporting EDI messages.
4. These three proxies were suggested by Fabio Leoncini, Managing Director of the luxury goods unit and member of the Board of Directors of Loro Piana, SPA—one of the world's most renowned luxury garment firms, specializing is custom-made cashmere production; he called his company a "tiny global luxury retailer".
5. Search Engine Optimization (SEO) involves making small modifications to parts of a website (content, keywords) that can have noticeable impact on a website's user experience and performance in organic search results on search engines, e.g. Google.
6. The brand name is a pseudonym.
7. Search Engine Marketing (SEM) is the process of gaining website traffic by purchasing ads on search engines.
8. Return on Investment.

BIBLIOGRAPHY

Aspers, P., & Godart, F. (2013). Sociology of fashion: Order & change. *Annual Review of Sociology, 39,* 171–192.

Bourdieu, P. (1993a). Haute culture and haute couture. In Bourdieu, P. (Ed.), *Sociology in question,* 132–138. London: Sage.

Bourdieu, P. (1993b). *The field of cultural production: Essays on art and literature.* Cambridge: Polity.

Bourdieu, P., & Delsaut, Y. (1975). Le couturier et sa griffe: Contribution à une théorie de la magie. *Actes de la Recherche en Sciences Sociales, 1*(1), 7–36.

Crane, D. (1997). Globalization, organizational size, and innovation in the French luxury fashion industry: Production of culture theory revisited. *Poetics, 24*(6), 393–414.

Crane, D. (2012). *Fashion and its social agendas: Class, gender, and identity in clothing.* Chicago: University of Chicago Press.

Edelman, L.B. (1992). Legal ambiguity and symbolic structures: Organizational mediation of civil rights. *American Journal of Sociology, 95,* 1401–1440.

Entwistle, J., & Rocamora, A. (2006). The field of fashion materialized: A study of London fashion week. *Sociology, 40*(4), 735–751.

Evans, C. (2014). The mechanical smile. *Fashion Theory, 18*(4), 479–492.

Geczky, A., & Karaminas, V. (Eds.). (2012). *Fashion and art.* Oxford: Berg.

Kawamura, Y. (2004). *The Japanese revolution in Paris fashion.* Oxford: Berg.

Laudon, K. C., & Traver, C. G. (2013). *E-commerce.* Pearson.

Meyer, J.W., & Rowan, B. (1977). Institutionalized organizations: Formal structure as myth and ceremony. *American Journal of Sociology, 83*(2), 340–363.

Mora, E. (2006). Collective production of creativity in the Italian fashion system. *Poetics, 34*(6), 334–353.

Pedroni, M., & Volonté, P. (2014). Art seen from outside: Non-artistic legitimation within the field of fashion design. *Poetics, 43,* 102–119.

Petkova, I. (2016). Between high-tech and high-fashion: How e-commerce fashion organizations gain moral and pragmatic legitimacy in the fashion field. *Poetics, 57*(August), 55–69.

Powell, W.W. (2012). Expanding the scope of institutional analysis. In DiMaggio, P.J., & Powell, W.W. (Eds.), *The new institutionalism in organizational analysis,* 183–201. Chicago, IL: University of Chicago Press.

Scott, W.R. (2008). *Institutions and organizations: Ideas and interests.* SAGE.

Selznick, P. (1949). *TVA and the grass roots: A study in the sociology of formal organization* (Vol. 3). Univ of California Press.

Selznick, P. (2011). *Leadership in administration: A sociological interpretation.* Quid Pro Books.

Shapiro, R., & Heinich, N. (2012). When is artification?. *Contemporary Aesthetics, 4,* 1–12. Retrieved April 5, from http://www.contempaesthetics.org/newvolume/pages/article.php?articleID=639.

Van de Peer, A. (2014). Re-artification in a world of de-artification: Materiality and intellectualization in fashion media discourse 1949–2010. *Cultural Sociology, 8*(4), 443–461.

Zajac, E.J., & Westphal, J.D. (1994). The costs and benefits of managerial incentives and monitoring in large US corporations: When is more not better? *Strategic Management Journal, 15*(S1), 121–142.

CHAPTER 4

The Evolution of Digital Moda as an Institutional Entrepreneur

We are vast and complicated.
Chief Executive Officer (CEO), *Digital Moda USA*
*We wanted to set up a company that is able to evolve in a way that, at a
certain stage in time, no matter what, it was able to succeed.*
Chief Commercial Officer (CCO), *Digital Moda*

The institutional emergence of *Digital Moda*, recounted by the Chief
Commercial Officer (CCO)—second in command at the company—
was initiated by "20 people in a basement with very limited connection
to the fashion system and with an idea". The line is intensely similar to
the stories of Internet pioneers, whose founders started in "garages"
(Amazon, Google), "dorm rooms" (Facebook), and "living rooms"
(eBay) before eventually becoming household brand names. The CCO,
who had been with *Digital Moda* since its inception in 2000, explained
that at the outset, the company had a twofold objective—perhaps in line
with the dual existence of fashion companies themselves as both aesthetic
and commercial entities—of both as "a *global* internet provider [...] *and*
a type of retail fashion company that is *different than mainstream retail*".
The three co-founders emphasized in their early discussions in 2000
that distinction from other e-commerce and brick-and-mortar retailing
models would be considered an important cultural competence as they
embarked on their path to legitimacy.

The deeply transformative cultural investment of the founders motivated the development of business competence in the emerging digital

© The Author(s) 2018
I. Petkova, *Engineering Legitimacy*,
https://doi.org/10.1007/978-3-319-90707-9_4

field of fashion, despite the fact that the company's CEO—who has stayed in this role for the past seventeen years—was neither in fashion, nor was he a technology expert. Having graduated in finance, he worked in consulting before calling it quits in 2000. "He dealt with a lot of fashion projects and is very fond of technology", the CCO noted, "but is fond of technology as a user. He was *outside of the fashion world*".

Digital Moda's founding team, nevertheless, embraced their outsider status and this may have been a crucial point in understanding the importance of creating narratives for legitimization that solidified the existence of the fledgling company in the fashion field. The key idea that the co-founders imparted was that "the Internet might be a game changer", as per the CCO:

> We were not exactly generating the change, because market effects and technology already generated the change. But, *maybe the possibility was there to helping the change to become real.* So, we set out to help fashion companies understand that change is occurring and how to face it. So, *the point is not so much how to replicate on the web what you already have. The point is to being the global Internet partner for these companies.*

As an emerging institutional entrepreneur in e-commerce fashion, *Digital Moda* focused on a cultural identity spanning many areas, instead of a single focus—acquire and sell fashion product—employed by previous competitors in the space, such as Bluefly. As the CCO's position above explains, the cultural goal of the future operator was much larger. *Digital Moda*'s founders conceived of their fledgling company as an "incubator of ideas for the *transitioning of the culture* of fashion brands online" (CCO). Not only did this goal necessitate that *Digital Moda* develop their own e-commerce capability, but also create an in-house e-commerce *division* that would ultimately launch an effort to *restructure retail and communications operations of fashion companies for the Internet.*

The CEO of the US office, based in NYC, and charged with exploring opportunities for generating innovative ideas in the surrounding Tribeca start-up and Silicon Alley area, explained that the founding team at *Digital Moda* decided to manufacture an identity that surpassed that of *Luxemod* or *Samplemod*, because the end goal was developing e-commerce capabilities for fashion companies:

> [*Luxemod*] only sells women's clothes, combining magazine and retail, and, *Samplemod* is an outlet for fast shopping. So, in this particular

situation we could actually refer to [*Luxemod*] as a digital or virtual whole-saler/magazine? They are also launching some white label stuff, like Jimmy Choo, but it's really small. *And we are vast and complicated.* We have more than one in-house E-Commerce brand. And then, we have 27 [fashion company] partner brands. They are both organized and served by different principles.

An important facet of *Digital Moda*'s internal narrative development was founders' hypothesis that in order to ensure established fashion compa-nies accept e-commerce as a legitimate new practice, e-commerce tech-nology should not be communicated as the bedrock of the business. Instead, the founding team should connect the value of online technolo-gies in e-commerce, marketing, social commerce, and social media, with both aesthetic and commercial goals; thereby, intellectualizing the prac-tice (Cronin 2004) in terms that were easier to understand in fashion companies. The Global Director of Marketing mused that this would not be a difficult goal to reach. Narratives for moral legitimacy at *Digital Moda* emerged contemporaneously with the development of actual capa-bility in e-commerce. "In 2000, when we started talking about digital marketing, we were talking about *digital marketing*", he underscored. "We never had an agency; we always created our main functions our-selves". We already observed that in comparison with other peers (Table 2.1), and as a direct result from the distinct focus of founders on partnering with fashion companies, *Digital Moda* was able to carve out dominant share of the developing competence in the field of digital fash-ion (Fig. 4.1). As the CCO exclaimed, when looking back at the very beginning of *Digital Moda*'s journey, "[w]e wanted to set up a company that is able to evolve in a way that, at a certain stage in time, *no matter what*, it was able to succeed". In short, *Digital Moda* had to effectively crosscut their "native" technical environment and plunge into the uncer-tain waters of persuading fashion company stakeholders of the social acceptability and moral fortitude of its activities and projects (Meyer and Scott 1983; DiMaggio and Powell 1983; Powell 2012a, b).

During the same year that *Luxemod* was launched (2000), *Digital Moda* founded its first branded e-commerce fashion property, *DigitalModa.com*[1] (Fig. 4.1). This branded property was conceived as a discounted e-commerce retailer—much like *Samplemod's* business model had taken off in 2007. The primary goal of *DigitalModa.com* was to acquire, market, and sell luxury fashion merchandise, sourced *directly* from high-fashion companies. This move was, furthermore, a strategic

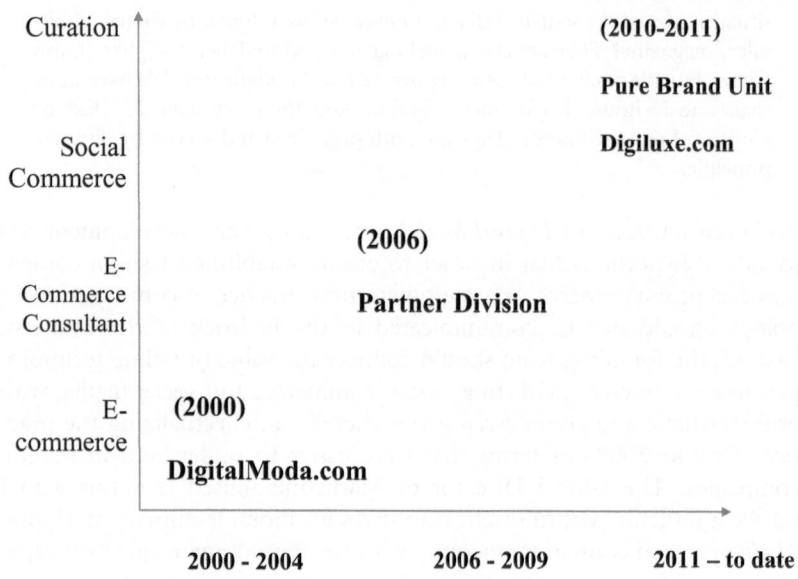

Fig. 4.1 Evolution in competence in *Digital Moda*

game for reaching deep into Communications and Retail—the two key decision-making units in European high-fashion brands. In 2006, *Digital Moda* created a new *Partner Division*, extending the menu of services offered to fashion company partners and formalizing its growing legitimacy in e-commerce consulting for fashion brands. After 2006, *Digital Moda* created the e-commerce businesses for more than a dozen fashion brands from Europe and the USA, and in 2009 opened a full-price branded e-commerce property, called *Digiluxe.com*.[2] *Digiluxe.com* featured curated pieces from current season collections of emerging and established fashion designers.

The difference was that while *DigitalModa.com* was launched as a discounted e-commerce website at a time when *Digital Moda* had only launched, *Digiluxe.com* was designed to broaden the pragmatic reach of the company in the fashion industry. Executives at *Digital Moda* in charge of this new e-commerce property selected emerging fashion designers with commercial potential and aesthetic ambition, and cultivated their visibility with Co-branding and curation projects. Furthermore, *Digiluxe.com* had a critical complementary goal.

Executives from *Partner Division* at *Digital Moda* liaised with merchandisers at *Digiluxe.com* to filter out emerging fashion brands with growing social following and upward sales, in preparation to building a standalone e-commerce website for these fashion companies.

Finally, in 2010, *Digital Moda* augmented its legitimacy in the fashion industry by starting *Pure Brand Unit*. As we will come to appreciate in the next chapter, the role of this unit was ambitious and the territory that *Digital Moda* wanted to explore in the fashion industry through it, was yet uncharted. *Pure Brand* had to persuade current high-fashion clients, for which *Digital Moda* created and operated e-commerce, to grant the unit exclusivity in managing yet another critical aspect of their institutional identity: the content of their digital marketing campaigns. Thus, *Digital Moda* was at the precipice of taking one step further, toward handling communications for fashion companies.

Institutional Emergence: Story-Telling Through Narratives for Legitimization

Despite the rich fabric of competing ideas for bringing established fashion companies to the fold of e-commerce, *Digital Moda* went through an array of legitimizing challenges shared by other peers, whose overwhelming intent at succeeding as outsiders was detailed in Chapter 2. Financial investment, or dearth of it, was one. As a start-up, *Digital Moda* had received limited financial assets in two rounds of financing, each totaling around $10 million. These two consecutive rounds were also used to create *DigitalModa.com*, the company's first branded e-commerce property.

As with most aspects of legitimization, the founders' idea to start a long excursion into becoming, as per the CCO, "the global partner for fashion brands", arose as an experiment. The founders anticipated that if the fledgling start-up acquired substantial quantity of apparel product directly from high-fashion brands, *DigitalModa.com* would be the entry point to gaining a toehold into the palazzo entranceways of Milanese and Parisian fashion brands. The Director of *Partner Division* explained the process for manufacturing of partner identity:

> Our initial idea was compounded by our next idea: to build a shopping web presence for them. Then, let's make them *evolve in the direction of perceiving* that their main asset is the content they generate and this asset can

be easily transferred to the Internet. This asset is also visual and this in addition makes it easily transferable.

The CCO recalled the difficulty of these initial steps in gaining credibility. "We could not just go to people like Armani and say; Mr. Armani, here is the money and this is the product we offer. If we did it, by the way, we would not have sold it. And, if we bought it, we would not have sold it, because we did not have a customer". The common problem of earlier models, like *Bluefly*, was lack of sustained legitimacy with the designer houses of Europe. *Digital Moda*'s executive board decided that an easier access point into these partners was to begin buying luxury fashion apparel from top-end brick-and-mortar retailers; the latter, as we know, were already collaborating directly with designer brands. Large retailers also frequently sold their excess inventory.

Part of the cultural success of *Digital Moda* is the geography of its incorporation—Milan, Italy—one of the largest markets for sourcing of fashion. The origin represented both a sourcing and a cultural advantage over earlier models and contemporary peers. "We had an advantage", one co-founder held, "because we started off in Italy, which is the Mecca of designer clothing. There are a lot of quality brands there that you don't necessarily find in the US". The CEO of *Digital Moda* USA concurred, "[…] probably of the 100 biggest retailers in the world, 20 or 30 are based in Italy. It is a highly fragmented market, and [we] had to use it".

An early advantage for the founding team was that the decision to inaugurate *DigitalModa.com* as a discounted e-commerce fashion retailer was a temporary approach. Even though *DigitalModa.com* was a discounted fashion retailer, buyers responsible for the selection of fashion apparel were to source product *only* from small, boutique-like brick-and-mortar retailers. This was a clean break from Bluefly's approach of buying discounted apparel from large off-price department stores, and, almost never directly from fashion brands. "If you do the retailers", said *Digital Moda*'s USA CEO, "you do not get the same quality of the final product. We did have one wholesaler, who helped us start out, but again, it was a high-quality partner and one of the oldest high-fashion companies in Italy had a major stake in them".

Acquiring quality assortment from the "right" partner was a critical first step for the fledgling e-commerce company. "Fashion retailers in Italy are *shopkeepers*", a senior officer in charge of merchandising at *Digital Moda* explained. "In Italy we did not have, like in France or the

US, the department store culture. You have probably more shopkeepers in Milan, than in the whole USA". Unlike the US-born *Bluefly*, whose management relied on standard purchasing agreements with large off-price retailers, *Digital Moda*'s buying team hypothesized (correctly, as it turned out) that establishing direct sourcing relationships with fashion companies hinged on the quality of curation for the fashion product displayed on *DigitalModa.com*. Furthermore, fashion buyers deliberated that whether the fashion product displayed was off-price or not, was not a deciding factor for future fashion company partners. Thus, the decision by the buying team to approach smaller boutiques in Italy as their initial sourcing partners. The Head of Global Buying explained that smaller fashion boutiques in Italy, in fact, taught merchandisers and buyers at the unseasoned start-up how to go about curating fashion product, having "*already done the selection for us, and you did not have to select anymore*".

After two seasons, equivalent to a fashion year, *Digital Moda* gained access to the merchandising departments of smaller high-fashion brands and started negotiations to acquire fashion merchandise *directly* from the companies. During this entry experiment, *Digital Moda*'s founders insisted that the culture of their small, discounted e-commerce property should be distinct from the existing acquisition tactics of large department stores. The Head of Global Buying explained that in all initial negotiations, the following legitimizing narrative would be communicated and explored:

> The idea was, *high fashion never dies*. I do not want to set up an outlet. We did not feature in our store online the original price point at which the product was sold in the stores. You are buying a dress from Alexander McQueen, which is *not* seasonal. Let's transmit to the final customer that when they are buying something, which is one season old, you are buying *something, which has a lot of content within it*. This helped fashion companies to be less afraid to sell us end-of-season merchandise.

The "partner who understands fashion as an art form", added the Head of Global Buying, happened to be a pertinent legitimizing narrative for *Digital Moda*. Fashion company *createurs* were being offered understanding and appreciation for the art form that they had always aspired to sustain. The proposition by the founding team that the original price of an item would not be revealed to online customers was a clear legitimizing win, as this tactic revealed a softer, aesthetically grounded appreciation for commercial fashion. Contemporary peers of *Digital Moda*, like *Bluefly*, according to one of co-founder, lacked these two explicit incentives and were, purportedly, "never able to buy anything from fashion companies directly because they were too aggressive". A significant share of e-commerce fashion retailers always revealed the original retail price of a fashion item. Furthermore, the visual approach of fashion retailers continues to be to slash the original retail price and display a lower one; thereby decreeing that the function of the retail price as a measure of luxury was outdated. *Digital Moda*, conversely, displayed a single, creatively constructed "*Digital Moda price*", never showing the original pricing of an item.

Digital Moda's founders found that Chief Executive Officers, Presidents, Merchandisers, and Head Designers at high-fashion companies appreciated the value of this legitimizing approach to expressing the very material properties of "fashion as art". This was markedly different from the legitimization practice of earlier approaches, as *Bluefly*. "Bluefly said", a co-founder at *Digital Moda* asserted, "we will give you *money* for your product. We said, we will give you *value*". During 2001, *Digital Moda* had acquired fashion product in excess of over 200,000 individual brand items. The company had created a niche in establishing legitimacy.

Aside from the original idea of defining price as a communicator of legitimacy, *Digital Moda*'s team deliberated that it was important to continually interpret how e-commerce technology can strengthen existing sources of value to fashion brands. As we discussed, both the lack of alignment between narrative and practice and proprietary e-commerce technology in eLuxury and Bluefly reinforced behaviors of complacency on the part of their founding teams. The latter believed that by mimicking the retail strategies by Neiman Marcus or Saks would result in gaining legitimacy with fashion companies. "They did not spend the money well on technology", the Chief Technology Evangelist (CTE) in the US office argued. "Instead of making an effort in strengthening the assortment, they invested a lot in advertising of poor assortment. When you address a fashion audience, you basically have to get the right assortment". Conversely, eLuxury gained legitimacy by relying on a superb assortment derived from direct relationships with LVMH's brands, but poor online communications and marketing. It "needed more *personality* and more character", the CCO of *Digital Moda* noted. "*You need to build content around what you sell*".

Digital Moda's CCO recalled in 2012 that even after the financial crisis hit in 2008, *Digital Moda*'s executive team theorized that the pragmatic legitimacy of the company might be compromised, if *DigitalModa. com* exploited vulnerabilities in fashion industry partners related to their financial status:

> The price positioning of Levi's in the US is half what it is in Europe. Why? It is because Levi's left the arena of quality. In a different way, on the Internet, this could happen to other fashion companies. If things go wrong, the Internet is highly competitive, customer-driven, and price-comparative. These guys[3] may be trickling down status. These things take out of exclusivity. And, *exclusivity* is why the fashion system works.

Executives at *Digital Moda* thought long and hard about the one key problem e-commerce might bring to fashion companies: the difficulty to convey what is exclusivity online. Unlike the brick-and-mortar fashion industry, where exclusivity was typically gauged by the distinctiveness of the retailer carrying the brand and the average value of a high-fashion item, determining exclusivity online was more complex. "What in the physical world is location", the Head of Global Buying at *Digital Moda* explained, "in the online world is traffic,[4] and the type of traffic that you generate, is the type of location you will have".

Digital Moda's CCO added that the key to operating in a technology-driven field for high-fashion companies was to integrate "right" assortment with suitable content. The CCO believed that only some of *Digital Moda*'s e-commerce peers "*understood the cultural significance of content creation*" for fashion companies. Successful peers, he suggested, had developed "a lot of content around the product" introduced on their website.

It was common that the team in charge of initial e-commerce negotiations with fashion companies at *Digital Moda* started out by outlining the emerging demography in e-commerce fashion by buttressing and weakening the position of various players. *Samplemod*, for example, was considered to be culturally beneficial as a model to the fashion industry. The narratives for legitimization pursued by *Samplemod* were aligned with *Digital Moda*'s own approach. Similar to *Digital Moda*, *Samplemod* had pursued moral and pragmatic legitimacy by creating narratives of an exclusive marketing channel for fashion brands and aligning these narratives with Co-branding and curation practices. The US Director of

Marketing at *Digital Moda* noted that the high-fashion orientation of *Samplemod* created visible recognition for this company and, as a result, this player was validated as a favorable platform for fashion companies. In short, *Digital Moda*'s executives (the Head of Global Buying in this quote) created an affirmative valuation for *Samplemod* by conceptualizing the company as a model that "gives the customer and the market very strongly the *message* that they are very good at what they do. There is the perception that they are telling a very nice story, a fairytale; and then, the real exclusivity".

Conflicts in acknowledging the legitimacy of other peers in the field arose for *Digital Moda* executives only when the team perceived that there was misalignment between "thinking" and "doing" in their e-commerce colleagues. In short, when the narratives for legitimization of other e-commerce actors did not correspond with the actual practice developed by them. *Digital Moda* executives were, for example, wary of supporting the legitimacy of *Vente-Privee*, a long-time competitor of *Samplemod*. *Vente-Privee* was a French company started in 2001 as a direct-to-consumer e-commerce model. The narrative for legitimizing *Vente-Privee* was initially focused around hosting of high-fashion brand sales for a members-only audience at deeply discounted prices. The company has, since, expanded in size and revenue: over €3.1 billion in 2016 (Agnew 2017). Despite the original scope of legitimization, in addition to fashion product *Vente-Privee* augmented the range of offerings with a variety of household products, such as appliances, electronics, and even *Vente-Privee* honey: all part of its daily sales model.

According to its founder, Jacques-Antoine Granjon, *Vente-Privee's* practice eventually became aligned with a pronounced mass sales approach: "You need something, you go to Amazon. With Vente-Privee, you need nothing but something in your head says: let's go and see if there's something fun, or if I can go and buy something cheaply" (Agnew 2017). Concerned with misalignment between *Vente-Privee's* narratives for legitimization and its actual practice, *Digital Moda* became apprehensive in evaluating the former positively. The merchandising team consequently clarified in their presentations to partner fashion companies that *Digital Moda*'s own path for legitimizing its practice contrasted sharply with *Vente-Privee's* model. Whereas the former was about exclusivity in curation and representation, the latter was about commodification of the fashion industry. Said the CCO:

If the model spreads, fashion will disappear as a concept. I think that [*Samplemod*] was just a bit inspired by *Vente-Privee* – a huge company. *Vente-Privee* is much bigger than [*Samplemod*]. They sell anything from refrigerators to Bottega Veneta, to Peugeot cars. With the Vente-Privee model the fashion will disappear, *because they are making fashion a commodity.*

Digital Moda's largest competitor in e-commerce fashion, *Luxemod*, received both praise and criticism. The CCO of *Digital Moda* argued that *Luxemod* deliberately tried to mimic the behavior of large retail department stores and this problem occurred because a co-founder at that company was ostensibly locked-in,

> *Entrenched* in a way of conceiving fashion and the Internet, in my personal perception, as conservative. I might be wrong, of course: the establishment conveys the idea that if things have been going this way for the last 50 years, maybe this is the way they should go. So, maybe [*Luxemod*] are completely right. But, what [*Luxemod*] have done on the web is in my personal perception, mainstream.

Executives at *Digital Moda* were particularly concerned with how to clarify to fashion brands "the cultural reasons why the consumer visits any particular online retailer" (CCO). The company was one of very few e-commerce fashion players to develop capability in designing and operating e-commerce properties for fashion companies. Nevertheless, describing to fashion partners how *Digital Moda* was an exclusive retail channel was difficult, because of overlapping narratives for legitimization between players in the field. The Director of Marketing attempted to explain exclusivity at *Digital Moda* as a proficiency in assortment (curation) of fashion product and price points. He frequently stressed measurable differences between known players in the field, neatly positioning *Digital Moda* as the focal point in e-commerce fashion:

> If you take our customer and you compare it with Saks and *Luxemod*, you may find similarity and overlap, but the reasons customers go to each channel are very different. *DigitalModa.com* – you are looking for assortment 60 per cent of the time and for price point, 40 per cent. Valentino.com, you are doing it even if you are the same person – for a different reason. If you buy, even Valentino, on *Luxemod*, you are doing it for selection, editorial, brand positioning. On Valentino.com, you are buying just

because you want to have the contact with the brand; something that *Luxemod* will never give you. From an objective standpoint, we are competing in the same arena, but we are fulfilling different needs for maybe sometimes the same customer.

ACQUISITION STRATEGY: BALANCING BETWEEN COMMERCIAL APPEAL AND AESTHETIC EXCLUSIVITY

The fashion brands that first agreed to sell their product on *DigitalModa.com* are two well-known high-fashion houses, with very different profitability and product lines, ranging from $50 million and $1 billion, in annual sales for 2011. As noted by the CIO at *MilanModal* in Chapter 3, in the 1980s large retailers had pushed for consignment agreements with fashion companies and this unilateral move had transferred merchandise risk to the latter. Breaking with this tradition, *Digital Moda*'s founding team did not want to push consignment on their initial clients. The CCO noted that the Head of Buying for *Digital Moda.com* intentionally negotiated that the very first acquisitions of fashion product from fashion companies will be in cash. This was a key decision in building trust with merchandising executives at fashion brands.

The Buying Director in the US office and the Head of Buying at *Digital Moda*'s headquarters in Italy observed that fashion companies had difficult time trusting that *Digital Moda* would successfully sell their discounted branded product online. Nevertheless, the Buying Director assessed that with each ensuing season fashion executives warmed to the idea of signing consignment deals in place of regular sales agreement. "Basically", she asserted, "our suppliers prefer the consignment *when they realize* that we are indeed going to sell very well. They *realize* that they would make more money with a consignment agreement". In only three regular fashion seasons, *Digital Moda*'s fashion partners, which had directly sold branded fashion product to the company, opened up to exclusive renegotiation of the terms to consignment. The former Global Head of Buying referred to the one-and-a-half year as "a crucial period in which we tried to *consolidate* the relationship". During this time, *Digital Moda*'s merchandising team in Italy nurtured emerging relationships with fashion brands by regularly communicating detailed data on product sales with them.

We can corroborate to the level of trust developed with local Italian companies by contrasting the lifecycle of merchandise acquisition with the US office, where *Digital Moda* established presence in 2007. From this vantage point, *Digital Moda*'s entry into e-commerce fashion in the United States provides a glimpse at how the company negotiated the challenge of legitimization in this new context. In Italy, the firm had successfully developed long-term buying contracts with fashion companies, and the approach to buying in that context had become more routinized and quantitative over the years. "In Italy", argued the Buying Director in the United States, "we have a 10-year experience, and so we have much bigger volumes, more numbers". Furthermore, *Digital Moda*'s buying team had graduated from having to sit through extensive negotiations with retail and communications departments in fashion companies in the early 2000s, to simply approaching logistics or warehouse managers for fashion product. In short, *Digital Moda* had acquired not only moral, but also pragmatic legitimacy in its country of birth, assessed by the ability of buying and merchandising to acquire, advertise, and sell branded fashion product.

In the United States, initially, *Digital Moda* did not have consignment agreements with fashion designers. The situation resembled a paradox. On the one hand, relationships with US fashion companies were cultivated by approaching their marketing or e-commerce teams *directly* (US fashion companies had been relatively open to the adoption of e-commerce). On the other, the buying team had to ascertain legitimacy to US fashion companies in the same manner that the company had done with European partners—by communicating *Digital Moda*'s narratives for legitimization and aligning them with actual practice. Mediated by the weakness of trust, the organizational structure of *Digital Moda* in the United States differed from the one at headquarters.

In Italy, the buying and the business development teams were separated. The buying team was started first. It was responsible for negotiations and acquisition of fashion product. The business development team emerged in 2006 and its main area of competence was to develop and maintain e-commerce properties for fashion companies. In the United States, both of these teams were integrated, in order to quicken the process of legitimization with US companies. *Digital Moda* buyers typically approached fashion company's sales team or, on rare occasions, the marketing team. The contact was established by attending trade shows, or by hiring consultants from the fashion industry with access to US fashion brands. "Once I have the appointment", said the US Head of Buying, "I try to *convince* them that we are the best. We preserve the image of the brand; we never slash prices. We never scream the brand name; it's a much softer process".

Acquisition and Pricing of Product in the United States: The 'Eyeballing' Rule

A quick look at how *Digital Moda*'s New York office decided on the acquisition and pricing of product acquired from US fashion companies allows to get a further glimpse into the development of actual practice at *Digital Moda* and observe how it aligned with the original narratives for legitimization at *Digital Moda* back in early 2000s. The approach to pricing of fashion merchandise acquired from US fashion companies was artisanal, painstakingly manual, and driven by assumptions of quality and exclusivity. This had been the precise legitimizing approach to gaining pragmatic legitimacy with European fashion houses. "We were the only people doing buying back then. There are a lot more now, but it's important to stay consistent", elaborated the US CEO at *Digital Moda*'s NYC office.

When *Digital Moda* opened its US office in 2007, the company competed in a context ripe with rivals. The team in United States was challenged to legitimize their moral and pragmatic standing in yet another fashion context. For at least three to four seasons, the acquisition-to-selling ratio of US fashion product remained historically low on *DigitalModa.com*. The US CEO remarked in 2010 that, "the problem is not in the [fashion] brand, but in *Digital Moda's brand*". The alignment between narrative and practice in the United States required creative approaches to becoming recognized by US fashion companies; approaches that *Digital Moda* had deliberately eschewed in Europe due to the sensitivity of European fashion companies to approaching e-commerce aggressively.

Whereas European high-fashion companies intentionally avoided exposure to online marketing strategies, including Co-branding, in the United States, fashion companies preferred what the US Director of Marketing called "banner-based push marketing" aimed at promoting precisely the *commercial* aspect of their fashion product. *Digital Moda*'s team began experimenting with banner advertising for fashion product acquired from US companies. However, the executive team in the United States remained insistent on proving that *Digital Moda*'s pragmatic skills extended beyond cherry picking of fashion product and its curation across multiple websites. *Digital Moda* had to convince US designers of its capabilities in directing their commercial path online. The first step was up to *Digital Moda*'s merchandising team in the United States, which became responsible for curating—aesthetically and commercially—fashion product from US companies. This task was not always easy and there were no guarantees that in two or three years consignment agreements with US companies would lead to commercial success for *Digital Moda*. It came down to trying and trust.

The Global Head of Buying at *Digital Moda* stressed that this legitimizing process had to be repeated with each new fashion partner. Trust had to be cultivated by communicating *Digital Moda*'s existing narratives for legitimization and further aligning them with current practice:

> Catherine Malandrino, Halston, Philip Lim, Proenza Schouler. [...] Sometimes, we need to work on developing the relationship. Some of them just have a lot of stock and they say – we know you, we'll give it to you. Others, like [mentions a well-known US fashion designer], we worked with them for two years. This brand is a small brand, but it is well distributed. I asked them for two years to sell me product, but they always said that they couldn't, since they have exclusivity agreement with other competitor, blah, blah, blah. In the end, fifteen days ago, they sold it to me.

At the start of the US expansion in 2007, the selection and pricing for acquired fashion product from local fashion companies deliberately began as a qualitative, artisanal process in which each item was priced manually. Pricing alone was a laborious process for a merchandiser. Recall, that part of *Digital Moda*'s legitimizing narrative was to ensure that selection and pricing of fashion items was based on a practice combining exclusivity (by demonstrating superb skills in curation) and heritage/timelessness (by being generous on pricing markups with brands). "For very local brands, I have to *try*", said the Head of Buying at *Digital Moda* in the United States; "I am not sure that it will sell, but if I see that it is very well distributed around; if I read Women's Wear Daily (WWD) and see many pictures with the brand's apparel... of course, you have to try... it is also a matter of *sensibility*".

Going through the list of recently acquired brands was done on an item-by-item basis, taking merchandisers eight hours at a time in 2012. The process of pricing included cataloging of orders at the warehouse level, reviewing merchandise codes, and setting pre-markdown '*Digital Moda* prices'. Pricing and curation were frequently done at the same time. As they priced fashion items, merchandisers in the United States also placed them under a relevant category on *DigitalModa.com*, pairing them further with similar fashion product and brand. With long-standing fashion partners, pricing was made on the basis of the merchandiser's instinct. A senior merchandiser explained that sometimes the team would "boot an item to a random price". This meant that the merchandiser will look at a picture of the product—just like a buyer would before choosing what to buy—and decide that, "if it is expensive, but looks 'naah', I will put a lower *Digital Moda* price on it".

Digital Moda's executives referred to this approach to pricing as an "eyeballing rule"; a complex selection process in which a merchandiser balanced between commercial appeal and exclusivity when setting prices on very expensive, premium brands. If very expensive brands, well-known or not, had low sell-through,[5] merchandisers suggested the markdown on the basis of their own feelings about the level of pricing that would make the brand commercially more appealing. Senior and junior merchandisers in the US office frequently met to discuss and "to double-check if the rate of markdown is perhaps really applicable to all [brands]". This ostensibly simple operation took no more than twenty minutes, yet every piece of merchandise from a particular brand that did or did not have high sell-through was carefully examined on a spreadsheet. The senior merchandiser may suggest that, "at this time, let's not have a target. Right now, we want to up the sell-through". The junior merchandiser may ask: "Is there normally a target?" The senior colleague would then suggest that the targeted price for a brand follows only one rule: "once you reach a critical mass, you have to pay much closer attention to the markdowns we apply".

Among the brands that occasionally experienced a low sell-through were some well-known European and US fashion brands (comparable to Thomas Meyer, Maison Martin Margiela, Mizrahi, Tom Ford, Jil Sander, CNC Costume National, Robert Rodriguez, Just Cavalli, etc.). Because fashion brands, as these, were very well known, merchandisers decided to keep them at a very low markdown. "Maybe the brand wasn't promoted enough, problem of selection, problem of pricing", a US merchandiser noted. Trial and error techniques based on merchandiser's instinct included starting a different promotional campaign with their marketing colleagues at *Digital Moda*, and in rare circumstances, ending the acquisition relationship with the fashion company. This level of detail was an important ingredient in cementing the relationship with *Digital Moda*'s first fashion partners in Europe. The attention to detail in brand acquisition and pricing in the United States allowed *Digital Moda* to achieve more trusted relationships with brands and generate momentum for advancing the partnership to the level of building and managing e-commerce, after testing the commercial and aesthetic potential of a fashion brand online.

NOTES

1. *DigitalModa.com* is a pseudonym.
2. *Digiluxe.com* is a pseudonym.
3. "These guys" is a reference to other e-commerce fashion retailers that exploited the financial vulnerabilities of fashion companies during the financial crisis, and more generally, between 2008 and 2010. As we learned in Chapter 2, Executives at *Digital Moda* aggressively compared their legitimacy narratives with the legitimacy narratives created by *Luxemod* and *Samplemod*, their two closest competitors. Even though their legitimacy narratives were close, *Digital Moda* considered that its own approach to addressing how to build exclusivity for fashion companies online was superior.
4. Traffic here is defined as the number of visitors on a particular online page and the number of pages related to an e-commerce property that they visit.
5. Sell-through is the percentage, comparing the amount of inventory a retailer (e.g., *Digital Moda*) receives from a supplier (e.g., fashion brand) against what is actually sold to the customer.

BIBLIOGRAPHY

Agnew, H. (2017). Jacques-Antoine Granjon has grand designs for Vente-Privee. *Financial Times*. Retrieved from: https://www.ft.com/content/e2c12042-1af0-11e7-a266-12672483791a [17 July 2017].

Cronin, A.M. (2004). Regimes of mediation, advertising practitioners as cultural intermediaries? *Consumption Markets & Culture, 7*(4), 349–369.

DiMaggio, P.J., & Powell, W.W. (1983). The iron cage revisited: Institutional isomorphism & collective rationality in organizational fields. *American Sociological Review, 48,* 147–160.

Meyer, J.W., & Scott, W.R. (1983). Centralization and the legitimacy problems of local government. In Meyer, J.W., & Scott, W.R. (Eds.), *Organizational environments: Ritual and rationality*. Newbury Park: Sage.

Powell, W.W. (2012a). Expanding the scope of institutional analysis. In DiMaggio, P.J., & Powell, W.W. (Eds.), *The new institutionalism in organizational analysis*, 183–201. Chicago, IL: University of Chicago Press.

Powell, W.W. (2012b). The organization of societal sectors, propositions and early evidence. In Powell, W.W., & DiMaggio, P.J. (Eds.), *The new institutionalism in organizational analysis*. Chicago, IL: University of Chicago Press.

CHAPTER 5

Digital Moda: Institutionalizing Legitimacy in the Fashion Industry

We had to find an easy touch point between Internet and fashion.
Director, *Partner Division, Digital Moda*

When executives at *Digital Moda*'s headquarters in Milan and at the US office explained how their moral and practical legitimation took shape with fashion companies, they often assessed the question by stating that fashion brands had "permitted" the company to become a legitimate partner. The marketing team in the US explained the development of moral and pragmatic legitimacy in launching and operating more than a two-dozen e-commerce businesses, as "the offering and acceptance of *help*". "What I know for sure", the CEO at the US office explained, "is that this business depends on the client; *whether they want more or less help* with managing the store. We provide them with a set of tools that allow them to be independent. But, *they are not experts in E-Commerce and we devise together a strategy for managing the online store*". The Global Director of Marketing added a commercial dimension: "we are offering to *help* the brands, as stipulated in the contract that we are signing, basically a percentage of sales generated online."

To "help" was an important rhetorical tool that *Digital Moda* utilized during those first discussions with fashion brands in 2006, when the business development team in Italy probed the openness of fashion companies to transitioning their operations and aesthetic repertoire to e-commerce. "It's a dual goal", explained the *Partner Division* Director—the unit in *Digital Moda* responsible for setting up e-commerce relationships with

I. Petkova, *Engineering Legitimacy*,
https://doi.org/10.1007/978-3-319-90707-9_5

fashion companies. This statement was a clear reflection of the complex nature of alignment work going on in *Digital Moda* when managing both moral and economic aspects of legitimacy with institutionalized fashion organizations (Suchman 1995; Deephouse and Suchman 2008).

The first goal was to create e-commerce viability and online revenue for fashion companies. The development of acceptable commercial practice (see Scardaville 2009) by *Digital Moda* buttressed its claims for economic legitimacy. A positive response to opening e-commerce from a relevant executive division in a fashion company meant that the potential partner was willing to accept the organizational legitimacy of a new value-laden dimension in its everyday practice. Fashion companies that were at the cusp of partnering with *Digital Moda* had to conceptualize commercial viability identically to how executives at *BritModa* looked at it; as a straightforward goal of making money online. The US CEO noted that this goal was not difficult to achieve with companies that were already selling their fashion product to *Digital Moda*. "They [the brands] have seen the *numbers*", he stated. "It's that simple".

The second goal of *Partner Division* in advising fashion brands on adopting e-commerce was to improve aspects of their aesthetic appeal and consumer brand awareness, through experimenting with online marketing on the new channel. Fashion companies had been struggling to manage these value-added activities away from brick-and-mortar retailers and publisher partners. *Digital Moda* executives presented the Internet as a new platform for "liberation of art and content" for fashion brands. *Digital Moda*'s founders, led by the CCO explained to their first partners in 2006 that the fashion industry is "by definition a content creator. Fashion companies are like media companies". The two goals were, of course, interrelated. *Digital Moda*'s legitimacy and subsequent foray into lasting normative influence would grow, if fashion companies accepted that a gradual process of integration between ritual and rationality—and, this, of blending between commercial and aesthetic goals—was to occur on the new channel (Meyer and Rowan 1977).

Typically, fashion companies concealed the profit-making aspects of their practice by approaching such key work repertoires, as pricing, in the service of aesthetic intent. Fashion companies charged high margins for their product to offset the extremely high costs demanded by their communications divisions to grow aesthetic intangibles related to company's creation myth, heritage, quality, and craftsmanship that went into the development and production of merchandise. *Digital Moda* executives hoped that they could charm fashion partners into selling their merchandise or accepting e-commerce with the reverse appeal. Any hesitations on the part of potential fashion partners would be offset by their exposure to novel communication techniques that reduced costs, and were more effective than, say, traditional communication techniques, such as ad placements in Vogue. The CCO of *Digital Moda* explained that this narrative appealed to the artisanal roots of industry leaders:

> The upside is exploiting and enabling content for your final customer in a way in which this final customer can understand. Like in any other industry, knowledge is the main way to better understand the value of what you are buying. For the fashion *industry, knowledge is transmitted through content*. Put the creator, the designer in contact with the final customer via this new channel. You have the unbelievable opportunity of buying a piece of art and dress up with it.

Between 2008 and 2010, luxury fashion companies were gradually exposed to (and some had accepted) presence on social media platforms, like Facebook. The element that warranted these technologies legitimacy was their vast social reach. In fact, notoriously distressed members of the French *maison* community, including *Hermes* and *Christian Dior*, gradually discovered that good things came from being owners of a Facebook page or running runway collections linked to social media via YouTube. Dior created one of the first *YouTube* virals, produced by bloggers. A former executive in charge of marketing at a French fashion house discussed with the CEO the merits for transitioning to a culture that took advantage of social media. He boldly argued that the idea of using social media was "to create buzz. And to create a buzz, you need to engage bloggers. If you do other things, like *classical* media, it's different. Online, bloggers are the key. And the way we did it, we invited [to Paris] personally 15 bloggers from USA, China, France. The *most important* Paris blogger—she came. We had a lot of things to explain about the maison. We spent 2 days with them." Eventually, traditional players, like *Dior*, had accepted social media platforms as "harmless", as one *Hermes* executive put it. Companies, such as *LVMH* Moët Hennessy Louis Vuitton SE and *Burberry* quickly followed suit, starting YouTube and Facebook projects.

This swift change of heart in fashion companies did not transpire when contemplating exposure to e-commerce. When *Digital Moda* founded its *Partner Division* in 2006, e-commerce was an unknown and complicated practice; an ordeal that no fashion house wanted to do first. The fashion industry had only recently been exposed to the "corporate website" concept. Corporate websites served as prime real estate online for informing the public about the history of a brand and any persuasive reasons regarding a company's "excellence" or "exclusivity". In short, for fashion companies to accept e-commerce, *a lot* of them had to do it together, thereby collectively conferring legitimacy to the practice.

A significant progress occurred when the Director of *Partner Division* reminded Italian fashion companies—soon to be pioneers in luxury fashion e-commerce—that this would not be the first time that they would take historic decisions. The narrative for legitimization pursued by the *Partner Division* reminded Italian fashion companies that in the 1980s, Italian brands, in particular, had fought to be independent from large retailers. As recounted by the Director of *Partner Division*:

> The first and only reason to adopt [E-Commerce] is—everybody is doing it. In the fashion business, this is the herd mentality. We accomplished it by bringing the brands their freedom. What do you want to deliver in terms of product image? [We asked] A department store is by definition a wholesaler with its own buying team defining what they want to buy. Online store is of course managed by the brands; it is they who decide what pieces they should put in the e-shop. They know that out of one particular exclusive dress, they may only sell 1 piece, but it is a way to convey a brand image.

The founding team's legitimating narrative to fashion companies rested on assurances that as social media and social commerce technologies continued to evolve, a fashion company's corporate website (the only online property that fashion companies had used before 2006) would contribute very little to their largest perceived asset—their brand value. The Director of *Partner Division* quickly sketched the idea that over time, social commerce would contribute over two-thirds of 'brand value' in fashion companies (Fig. 5.1). An e-commerce property was, obviously, part of this sketch; for, without e-commerce, the Director of the *Partner Division* reasoned, there would be no logistical vehicle for fashion companies to enjoy the aesthetic and economic advantages of social commerce. E-commerce was an enabling technology, after all—argued the Director of *Partner Division*—through which highly curated fashion content could be made available instantaneously to selected publics.

Fig. 5.1 New practices as innovation vehicles for fashion companies

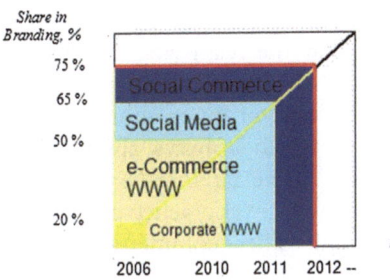

For example, an updated data feed of a company's latest fashion product could be made immediately searchable on search engines. The fashion product could be paired with editorial content and further incorporated into marketing campaigns promoted on social media and social commerce websites. As time went by, the idea of e-commerce was easier to sell, after executives in future fashion company partners learned in negotiations about the anticipated advantages from linking curated e-commerce fashion product with social commerce partnerships. In other words, *Digital Moda*'s *Partner Division* team fueled positive expectations in fashion partners regarding the likely broadening of their marketing and brand-related messages to new audiences.

The stigma of e-commerce was going to lift, eventually. Despite apprehension and lack of e-commerce experience, the CCO was confident that "fashion companies were, in fact, able to understand the market beyond marketing". What they had forgotten, added the US CEO at *Digital Moda*, was that their "*real* audiences were customers [who] judged the quality of their product every season" and that one of the roles of e-commerce would be to remind consumers of that function.

Seeking Moral Legitimacy in the Fashion Field

Digital Moda made specific choices regarding which brands to approach to explore the legitimacy of e-commerce. Generally, the executive team listed two main problems that could have inhibited future fashion partners from signing an e-commerce agreement. The first was to create a viable conversation by advancing narratives for legitimization that enabled fashion brands to think operationally and in terms of commercial decisions and results. "Despite the fact that you are very visionary company and a very visionary designer", recalled the CCO when explaining how the team went about deciding on this initiative, "the Internet would expose you to the customer in a way that you've never experienced before; much more deeply than a store or an advertising campaign, which is always, always, always executed with *no* clear achievement offline". The *Partner Division* Director rationalized that this problem of accepting novel practice and behavior stemmed from the fact that, as we learned earlier, commercial practice was typically obscured by aesthetic intent:

> The fashion system works with an advertising budget, which is set up to work with very high mark-ups and margins. The unsold products sold at a lower mark-up can easily cannibalize the brand perception and your ability to mark-up your product for lifetime. The fashion houses were very careful not to lose brand equity. This was the swift way for us to do it. *We had to find an easy touch point between Internet and fashion.* There was a way to selling fashion online, which actually protected the brand and protected the merchandise.

The second challenge for *Digital Moda*'s team was to convince fashion companies, having gained insight into the set up their organizational borders, to loosen the long-standing, siloed separation between retail and communications. The CCO hypothesized that to overcome this challenge, fashion company partners had to divest from their institutional promotion of aesthetics and invest in commercial logic:

> If you look at it from an organizational chart perspective of a fashion house in Italy, above certain percent, you will find that there are no Marketing Directors around, in *Armani* or *Gucci*. It's something I could never believe once I'd seen it. Marketing direction of *Dolce & Gabbana* is basically in charge of identifying the price point of products of comparable brands. Everything for *Gucci, Armani, Dolce & Gabbana* – what a company would call Marketing, they call Communications. I'm Gianni Versace. I never actually care if you prefer white dress or a black dress, because I am the maker of the dress. But, why should I hire a Marketing Director? I just need to hire someone to communicate you my vision of things. That is the way they see it.

In order to persuade fashion companies that their operational context was well understood, *Digital Moda* established its own PR and Communications team in the early stages of the development of its e-commerce consulting capability. The Director of PR and Communications was based in Italy along with eight other communications executives located across Europe, China, Japan and the USA. The launch of the new unit allowed *Digital Moda* to lobby for credibility in being perceived as representing "similar" identity to that of European high-fashion companies. This is how the Director General of *Fondazione Altagamma* validated *Digital Moda*'s enabling role, alluding to the similar "thinking" of these improbable—at first glance—categories of partners:

> The founder and his crew share the same culture of the luxury company. I believe that to meet the need of a high-fashion company, you need to be part of the same culture. They are not people dealing with just logistics and just with IT. They have the ability of defining the technical solution, but on top of that they share the vision and fully understand the needs of the fashion company, in terms of quality and service that has to be provided.

As executives at the *Partner Division* were drafting the critical points of future negotiations with fashion companies in 2006, the founding team made their work difficult by hypothesizing that the final decision on product selection for the e-commerce properties of fashion brands might be left to *Digital Moda* merchandisers, and not to fashion company employees. *Digital Moda* merchandisers were developing their complex "eyeballing" selection process, successfully balancing between commercial appeal and exclusivity when setting prices for premium fashion brands. To leave the final decision on product curation to *Digital Moda* could have far-reaching consequences that left the option for backlash from future partners open. Fashion company merchandisers could be expected to argue that only certain fashion categories and products should be put online, for instance, because they represented a seasonal highlight. "So they would be affected", said the US CEO, recounting his answer to internal discussions in 2006, in which company co-founders pondered how to go about e-commerce negotiations, if their future partners pushed for less commerce, and extra aesthetic presentation of product. The US CEO had developed an answer that seamlessly integrated between commercial and aesthetic goals and the existing institutional logic of fashion companies:

> The biggest challenge was to let people understand that the online store was another sales channel and it was not going to cannibalize their product

in other channels [...] the beauty of being online is that you only see one article; you never see racks of things. Buying 100,000 pieces of a t-shirt that the designer thinks is ugly *does not tantamount to putting them all on a rack*. Further, we can complement the item with other, more popular pieces from the collection; like, a $10,000 dress that the designer loves, but we'll only stock 2 pieces of it. So, that resolves the unseemly commercial problems that could be had in a physical store.

Knowing these counterarguments in advance actually facilitated early partnership choices by *Digital Moda* executives. The *Partner Division* Director, ever the driver of visual ideation, together with the CCO sketched out his arguments that the probability for fashion companies to partner with *Digital Moda* was going to recede as their annual turnover increased (Fig. 5.2). The number of companies in the fashion industry that operated in the $1 billion segment of the 'pyramid' was less than 20. *Gucci, Christian Dior, Vacheron Constantine, Chloe, Louis Vuitton*, and *Hermes* were some of these brands. They tended to be publicly listed and owned by diversified holding groups. One example was PPR, a French multinational holding company that has considerable shares in luxury fashion brands, as Brioni (100%), Gucci (100%), Yves Saint Laurent (100%), Sergio Rossi (100%), Boucheron (100%), Bottega Veneta (100%), and Alexander McQueen (51%).

The CCO also observed that when fashion brands were positioned in the lower tier of what he called "the openness to creativity" pyramid (Fig. 5.2), with annual revenue of less than $500 million, they tended to be privately owned and bolder in their design decisions, as well as communications and retail distribution choices. Lastly, when fashion companies got to the midpoint in the segment, they tended to have communications divisions in place, which complicated their internal levers of control. Fashion brands positioned at the lower point typically

Fig. 5.2 Inverted "openness to creativity" pyramid

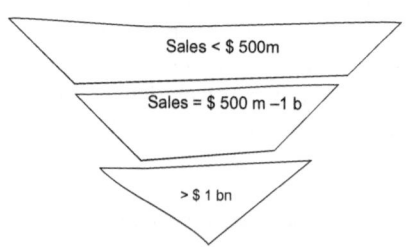

did not have communications or marketing direction. These were crucial cultural data for *Digital Moda*.

"Once in a while, you trim your distribution; you want the highest quality, most exclusive distribution. This is necessary, but it cuts your revenue", the CCO sketched out the difference in thinking between fashion firms with high and low turnover and their propensity of embracing new strategic decisions:

> So, what do you say to your shareholders? Well, the designer thought that adding the product in this direction is not so good for the brand, but the shareholder says: 'fire the designer'. If you are Burberry, *you are not anymore in the position of being pure.* You need to make compromises. I am sure that in the head of Christopher Bailey or the Marketing Director there is saying: would be nice to have the product just presented the way I want. But, how do I explain this to the analyst? If you are on the top, you already will have too much to compromise and this will reflect your Internet strategy.

The CCO would eventually posit to the executive team that smaller high-fashion brands, which tended to not have marketing divisions, could be more open to organizing by looking at e-commerce as a strategic commercial and aesthetic decision. The goal became to find a representative sample of high-fashion companies, brave enough in their decisions and having little, if any, experience in marketing/communications, or e-commerce. These potential partners were interesting to *Digital Moda* also, because their founders tended to micromanage operations, but were forthcoming generally and "tended to sort of tell you what you want to know" (Global Director of Marketing). The CCO suggested choosing fashion brands from the $500 million bracket for introducing e-commerce capability. The expectation was that, if a critical mass of smaller fashion brands decided to collaborate with *Digital Moda*, there would be a positive peer response from larger fashion brands. From a conceptual perspective, it also appeared that pragmatic legitimacy was easier to achieve, since *Digital Moda* had already gained moral legitimacy in the fashion field.

From 2006 to 2012, *Digital Moda* focused on collaboration with fashion companies positioned at the bottom of the pyramid. The majority of these companies were the prêt-a-porter fashion houses of Italy. They tended to be tightly knit in localized associations and, thus, easier to accept word-of-mouth from their peers. *Digital Moda*'s first e-commerce client was a smaller, well-known Italian luxury fashion company, which did not have a marketing director and whose owner (also, CEO) was enthusiastic in developing the digital identity of the brand, including, learning how to choose and update fashion product in the digital field. When *Digital Moda* entered the US market in 2007, the company was able to capitalize on its European reputation by gaining the trust of three US fashion brands that had won CFDA's *Designer of the Year* award in 2010 and 2011. By 2012, *Digital Moda* had achieved an important milestone. The company launched a joint venture partnership dedicated to managing e-commerce and online marketing for several luxury brands owned by a luxury conglomerate. The acquisition of moral and pragmatic legitimacy had finally paid off.

Gauging the Moral "Fit" for Collaboration

The first step in investigating the potential of e-commerce partnerships between *Digital Moda* and prospective fashion companies was a qualitative analysis of the "message" and the "image" of a brand. These two variables related to evaluating the retail distribution channels in which the brand was present and the content of marketing campaigns, if any, that were implemented by communications or marketing divisions. The team considered if the fashion company had a corporate website and how it was used. When a potential partner had no e-commerce, but otherwise, exhibited growing attachment to 'softer' activities online, such as digital runways, or support for bloggers and social media, the prospective relationship increased in importance, because the fashion company was engaging in experimenting.

The other step in the analysis of partners was to revisit the commercial aspect of collaboration by way of gauging how the average purchase value made by a fashion brand in brick-and-mortar stores where it was carried, stack up against the expected "average ticket" that would be generated by way of its own e-commerce. This quantitative exercise allowed to forecast if the partnership would be commercially beneficial to both partners, once the e-commerce website of a fashion brand was up and running. The average sales ticket was an important measure for the overall value of a fashion brand. The CEO of the US office recounted that "the average ticket will tell you *what sort of merchandise assortment the client actually sells*. When you get the information about average ticket, you already know what the brand stands for in terms of proposition; *what is the value of the brand.*"

In this manner, *Digital Moda* determined that its narratives for legitimization must align with the expectations of fashion industry partners that components of heritage, quality, and craftsmanship were the very first points to address in negotiations. The CEO at the US office explained that when seeking positive response from fashion companies, the legitimizing rhetoric in the *Partner Division* had to clearly communicate long-term, cultural benefits for both partners. Unlike other companies that required the payment of an annual fee for developing e-commerce websites for businesses, *Digital Moda* emphasized that revenue justification was not its only goal and that potential fashion partners should be willing to achieve mutually beneficial goals. Said the US CEO:

> I will be your partner for the online store, but if you do not reach some pre-specified minimum level of turnover, which justifies for me the percentage of revenue share, I will charge you anyway a minimum amount of money on a yearly basis to justify my revenue share with you. We don't do this. When we define a brand not strong enough in terms of potential annual sales online, we do *not* go ahead with a business plans.

Gauging the alignment of culture for both partners was a significant step to signing an agreement of withdrawing from one. Through conversation that centered on the aesthetic and commercial intent of the partnership, the next step was to sign a long-term contract, in which the partner agreed to adopt *Digital Moda*'s proprietary e-commerce technology and partnership model. *Digital Moda*'s Chief Technology Evangelist (CTE), who was positioned at the US office, recounted that the success of a relationship rested on the degree of prior moral legitimacy that the company had already gained with a potential partner. In short, the existence of prior moral legitimacy was a lever toward achieving pragmatic legitimacy. Even when fashion companies did not question the commercial approach of *Digital Moda*, the need for an alignment in culture represented by moral legitimacy had to be present, argued the CTE:

> We have developed our [E-Commerce] platform ourselves. We always saw a business as complex as *Digital Moda*, in terms of inventory management, flexibility in the management of pricing, different markets, different payment options, is something that is not easily found in E-Commerce,

meaning that you cannot find it in as flexible form as you may wish for a business as *Digital Moda*. *Something that changed the field completely* is when we extended our platform to take care of fashion company e-shops in a completely separated way in a logical sense, but using the same culture, and a successfully tested platform.

That platform for experimentation, of course, was *DigitalModa.com*, the first and largest e-commerce property of the company. *DigitalModa.com* was designed to be "[our] biggest brand, and we treat it as any other fashion E-Commerce brand" (CTE). This narrative for moral legitimacy aligned well with how *Digital Moda* desired to be perceived by its future fashion partners. Moreover, *Digital Moda*'s executives were constructing an *internal* narrative of cultural proprietorship over the Internet businesses of high-fashion partners by considering each of their partners' commercial websites to be *products* and *divisions* of *Digital Moda*. "We call our fashion partners' [E-commerce] websites, *our* websites," the CTE observed, "and the online stores that we have are basically *our* divisions".

ACHIEVING PRAGMATIC LEGITIMACY: THE PARTNER DIVISION

In 2006, one of Europe's youngest, most coveted luxury fashion brands signed an agreement with *Digital Moda* for the development of their first online store. In 2007, a prêt-a-porter clothier agreed to be *Digital Moda*'s second partner. When the first several e-commerce properties for luxury fashion companies were developed, *Digital Moda*'s founding team decided that the future would deliver enough fashion business to warrant the building of a new organizational unit to deal with the evolving expertise and pragmatic legitimacy. The institutionalization of this competence in e-commerce consulting was completed only after the executive team became "very strongly internally convinced" (according to the CCO) that *Digital Moda* could create practices in e-commerce that would fit the concerns of fashion companies.

The Marketing Manager at the US office argued that pragmatic legitimacy would ultimately be easier to achieve. This key conclusion rested on the observation that while fashion "mega brands have resources to free for an instrument like E-Commerce, they would have no time to reflect on the *consequences* of carrying out this instrument, and also on the possibility of designing the instrument on their own."

By establishing the formal organizational boundaries of the new practice with the founding of the *Partner Division, Digital Moda*'s executive team was institutionalizing an emerging competence on the road to pragmatic legitimacy.

The *Partner Division* was founded in 2006 and *Digital Moda*'s technology team played key role in conceptualizing the organizational model of the new division. One of the challenges in the process was to balance the limited headcount across the company in meeting potential demand. The *Partner Division* was initially comprised of only three people. One was in charge of technology and, per the CTE, "[...] two more were developers, broad skilled ones. And, by the end of the project, it was four people." Having served with the company since its founding in 2001, the CTE recalled the role of creative recombination in opening the division—"we took something from business development, project management, and technology and these integrated decisions provided the focus that was needed to make this project start." The new unit was an uncharted cultural dimension at *Digital Moda*. Throughout 2006, the executive team continued to advocate for an alignment of roles and practices developed in the new division with existing boundaries of moral legitimacy by *Digital Moda* in the fashion field. This was going to be another trial and error approach. "That unit [*Partner Division*] was a concept that was not present before in digital fashion", the CTE explained the importance of the undertaking, "and we had to change things in order to *add the concept of division for* fashion brands".

Digital Moda founders faced an unusual situation in constructing the *Partner Division*. The core technology team at the company had been shaped prior to developing the idea of creating e-commerce properties for fashion clients. The role of the technology team was broad and significant throughout *Digital Moda*, because tech was the core concept nurturing all other units at *Digital Moda* with skills in e-commerce and online marketing. The founders hypothesized that the technology team could leverage increasing demand from fashion companies, as long as the emerging *Partner Division* grew organically and learned to handle demand on its own.

Digital Moda's *Partner Division* had to work in tandem with the core technology team in creating an e-commerce solution that fitted the internal organization of companies with much smaller operations and catalogs than *DigitalModa.com*, the company's largest e-commerce fashion retailer. Furthermore, the challenge for the fledgling *Partner Division* was to act as liaison with their high-profile clients in aligning the existing cultural expectations of fashion executives to the actual e-commerce solution. The *Partner Division*, therefore, acted as an organizational intermediary, legitimizing the toolset of *Digital Moda* in e-commerce consulting in the quest for achieving pragmatic legitimacy.

Digital Moda's CTE recalled that "we had tools, but they were not relevant to be used for different stores and by people who did not have knowledge of internal rules in *Digital Moda*. They [the tools] had to be smoothed around the edges before we could expose them to the client." Among the main concerns of fashion company executives was the prospective "dilution" of status for their brands online. The immediate emphasis of the *Partner Division* during negotiations, appropriately, was to introduce e-commerce as an aesthetic practice that, through the role of web design, was able to communicate "the art of the brand". Commercial goals were introduced concurrently with focus on aesthetics.

Today, what used to be called 'mini-division' at headquarters in Milan has grown to be the largest organizational unit in *Digital Moda*. The *Partner Division* (Fig. 5.3) developed three distinct areas of expertise: e-commerce partner management, comprising of dedicated Partner Managers, who analyzed day-to-day e-commerce operations for a specific fashion partner; merchandising and curation officers that originally had the ability to select fashion product for the client's e-commerce property; and editorial content development team, which created and promoted editorial content for partner' e-commerce websites.

Acquiring pragmatic legitimacy for all of these featured practices was extremely valuable to *Digital Moda* founders. The US merchandising team, as we observed, had developed the complex "eyeballing" selection process, when setting prices for premium fashion brands and

Fig. 5.3 Partner division at *Digital Moda* (*Source* Internal documents. Simplified organizational structure)

a legitimization of this principle was advantageous to the company. The editorial content team originally engaged in editorial content creation. In early partnership agreements, this practice had to do with the design of editorial content for promotional newsletters, periodically sent to registered email users. Newsletters typically promoted new fashion collections or announced special campaigns. Legitimization of this practice would eventually help *Digital Moda* to manage growing portion of the digital budget for fashion companies and engage in increasingly complex projects for fashion company partners, such as Co-branding.

The process of building an e-commerce website was kicked off by holding high-level negotiations between *Digital Moda* and the fashion company. The early phases of negotiation featured *Digital Moda*'s CCO and Head of Business Development, on the one hand, and CEO or General Manager of the fashion brand, on the other. The CCO accentuated the absence of representatives from technical teams, such as Chief Technology Officer (CIO), at these negotiations. "The project is not generated by the CIO", he said. "Sometimes you've got the founder, the Commercial Director, and sometimes, people from Marketing." The organizational roles that the parties chose to kick-off negotiations exposed how important it was for fashion companies to assess the aesthetic viability of the new channel.

A noteworthy formalization of the relationship—and thus, realization of pragmatic legitimacy—occurred with signing of the e-commerce agreement. The fashion partner authorized *Digital Moda* to design and run their e-commerce property. Upon creating e-commerce, *Digital Moda* likewise assumed responsibility for running Search Engine Marketing (SEM) campaigns for improving the marketing positioning of the brand online. Fashion partners further agreed to reinvest a share of their annual revenue from e-commerce to finance other, *new marketing activities* that *Digital Moda* could stipulate at a later time. The contract, finally, dictated that *Digital Moda* would provide a "Partner Manager" in charge of e-commerce, *if* the fashion partner needed to have one. As we established earlier, experience with most partners indicated that even though the contract terms called for the recipient company to "have to hire an E-Commerce manager, if an E-Commerce manager is absent, this function is fulfilled by an *Internal Partner Manager* at *Digital Moda*" (CEO, USA).

When fashion partners opted to assign internal responsibility for e-commerce, they chose a remarkably diverse group of functions in their organizations. Across the board, positions such as Business Development

Manager, Brand Director, Owner/CEO, Commercial Director, and even Creative Director, were nominated to lead their fledgling e-commerce businesses. A concern materialized in *Digital Moda* headquarters. The diversity of appointees indicated that, without guidance, fashion partners might stall operational involvement in commercial or marketing activity related to running their new online businesses, and instead, turn the new practice into a *ritualized committment*. The *Partner Division* team, thus, moved to introduce two levers in the management of e-commerce for fashion partners; the first, represented by a Partner Manager at *Digital Moda* (one for each fashion company partner), and the second, ask for the introduction of an e-commerce director title and unit in partner companies. The *Partner Division* Director explained that this approach helped institutionalize e-commerce in fashion company partners and develop further pragmatic legitimacy at *Digital Moda*:

> We can't really figure out a way in which we can understand each other in terms of what exactly a Partner Manager does. Basically, [*Digital Moda*] and the brand should do the things that they are individually best at doing. They [Partner Managers at *Digital Moda*] should tendentiously do SEM, and should be guided by the brand. The brand, on the other hand, knows what they sell best. [...] They should also consistently liaise with our Partner Manager in order to develop the creative side of the partnership, such as banners and newsletters, done by us.

To ensure that fashion company partners aligned their existing organizational structures with the new e-commerce practice, Partner Managers and merchandisers at *Digital Moda* were continually involved in *jointly* choosing product assortment with merchandising directors at fashion company partners or, in the rare cases when those existed, with e-commerce heads for the company. The objective of collaboration at this initial stage was for Partner Managers at *Digital Moda* to act more like *retail* managers, rather than *digital* managers in order to ease fashion companies into accepting e-commerce as a pragmatic activity. In this setup, both sides collaborated on choosing fashion product assortment that would work online and harvest favorable sales results.

The other important part of the work for Partner Managers done jointly with editorial content and creative campaign staff was to produce *creative assets* for fashion partners, mainly e-newsletters. Electronic newsletters were a leading step into gaining pragmatic legitimacy for creatively driven assets in which both aesthetic and commercial intent was present. In *Digital Moda*'s own in-house experience with *DigitalModa.com*, newsletter campaigns contributed significant share of sales—10–30%. "It is insane not to use them", the Global Marketing Director argued. "The rationale for adding this activity with brands on top of the more basic SEM is because newsletters are *vehicles* for branding and selling in the end. The brands approve all of them and in some cases, they make them themselves."

It took many hours of web design and editorial work to create and editorialize the weekly newsletters for more than twenty fashion company partners in 2011. Each fashion company partner typically sent out one to two newsletters each week, featuring professional photography, endorsed "look of the week", tailored product offerings, and promotions. The more than twenty newsletters were further localized into seven languages—one for each localized e-commerce property of the fashion partner. The total count of editorialized e-newsletters came up to around 210 a week. This was a large-scale operation in content creation, because promotional content and product obviously had to be differentiated by brand. It is important to note that producing e-newsletters took a lot more creative labor in comparison to the routinized, quantitatively driven SEM activity, which was typically handled by no more than two people in the *Partner Division.*

Taking on a merchandising curation role and an editorial role was a challenge and an opportunity. As we observed in Chapter 3, European fashion companies had a setup where digital activities were either nonexistent until 2012, or larger fashion companies would have Creative or Communications Divisions, and these approved all content related to both paper-based and digital channel. The US CEO argued that institutionalizing the *Partner Division* and Partner Managers as the "*most relational* department and role that we have aside from the buying department" was a powerful move. It assured that fashion partners would have daily interaction with Partner Managers, who wore more than one hat. They were warehouse experts, coordinating deliveries from fashion brands to local warehouses. They acted as fashion merchandisers, taking responsibility for curating merchandise on partners' websites and updating sizes, styles, and content. Partner Managers were an extension of *Digital Moda*'s moral and pragmatic legitimacy in the fashion field. As per the Global Director of Marketing:

They are the point of the brand entrance; like account managers they do *relationship management: internally and externally.* We can see that each of our Partner Managers has unequal amount of fashion company partners underneath. But, this is an example of how we've *organically* evolved to build the company around people, as opposed to vice versa. The most that we do is having 2 people per website. *It is important to get one person that is the one that our partner trusts.*

The merchandising role of Partner Managers was particularly noteworthy in the context of pragmatic legitimacy for the digital channel. The role of digital merchandisers mirrored the growing clout of brick-and-mortar merchandisers in fashion companies. The difference was that the former curated fashion product directly on a fashion company's e-commerce website, rather than influence the design of upcoming collections. "Obviously," said a senior executive who took charge of merchandising for the US office, "you can't tell your partner, as a traditional merchandiser in a fashion company, would, 'hey, next season buy a little bit more than the last season'. The job of merchandisers here is to propose curation, sales budget, markdowns, and plan assortment on the web."

The relational role of Partner Managers was not without ambiguity on their part regarding the nature of their own work. The Marketing Director in the US noted that Partner Managers had less patience with fashion brands that were "exceptionally slow" in maintaining their everyday work routines. In meeting with Partner Managers, the Director of the *Partner Division* also noticed some confusion on behalf of the group with regard to "exactly what the 23 E-Commerce persons from the brand do on the other side?" The majority of fashion partners that had appointed internal managers for e-commerce appeared to show outward support for the new practice. However, when Partner Managers attempted to liaise with newly hired e-commerce team leaders on the other side on, say, problems with the conversion of digital traffic to sales, the latter rarely offered a response to remedy the problem. In short, these new hires would accept the onus of their new position, but did little to engage with the imperatives of actual work practice.

This was not altogether unexpected. Executives at headquarters understood that preference for partners with little to no knowledge of e-commerce may have backfired. These, otherwise "ideal", types of partners had to be influenced to trust their work practice on a daily basis. Between 2010 and 2012, fashion partners tended to pull existing workforce on the retail side of the business to head the new e-commerce units. The situation was not ideal for *Digital Moda*'s *Partner Division*, because a retail executive would seldom arrive with ideas that understood or supported e-commerce and online marketing. Subsequent to these new insights, merchandising, editorial, and management executives in the *Partner Division* decided that the role of Partner Managers would shift somewhat from helping introduce and design a new practice to *influencing* the direction of e-commerce within the fashion partner, such that a buy-in from digital executives on the other side was guaranteed. "In the ideal case", the US CEO speculated, "this person that is now in charge of E-Commerce [...] knows the right people to talk to about marketing budget and merchandising products. They have understanding of the product and the marketing side and are internally well-connected."

Partner Managers at *Digital Moda* were the chief protagonists that introduced practices related to gaining influence legitimacy into the relationship with fashion brands. The CEO of *Digital Moda* USA, who once held a Partner Manager role at headquarters, noted that the decision to influence the direction of discourse regarding e-commerce at the level of the fashion partner was the key approach to moving one step further from pragmatic legitimacy and gaining influence legitimacy. With this approach, Partner Managers combined their actual role of liaison and coordination with promoting the value of e-commerce practices as favorable to partner company goals:

> We thought that there should be only one [Partner Manager] per client because the [Partner Manager], in a sense, kind of *becomes* the brand; becomes the brand ambassador. That is even reflected in the way they dress. They instinctively know what the brand likes. There is of course a dialogue and they translate the outcomes from this discussion as a request to the content teams and the producers at *Digital Moda*.

As the experiment of gaining influence for the value of e-commerce practice with fashion partners went on, group executives began discussing in mid-2011 whether partner brands would accept an increasingly specialized menu of solutions in e-commerce from *Digital Moda*. Along with maintaining their engagement in SEM, the *Partner Division* began introducing new elements of collaboration with brands that were already tested on *Digital Moda*'s two other in-house brands, *DigitalModa.com* and *Digiluxe.com*. These new activities were related to more creative involvement in curation and Co-branding with social commerce companies, and in driving sales by promoting 'affiliate' programs to fashion company partners. Affiliate Marketing was a popular performance-driven initiative, in which one or more 'affiliated' websites, engaging in a promotion of a particular campaign at a partner website, would be remunerated for each visitor they brought to another e-commerce website by the affiliate's own marketing efforts.

However, as we established in Chapter 3, fashion companies had difficult time accepting these types of performance-based initiatives or partners. To counter possible opposition, Partner Managers initially decided to probe softer initiatives in social media outreach for fashion partners. The CCO recalled discussing with *Digital Moda*'s founder ways in which to point partner brands in the direction of accepting an integrated approach, in which *Digital Moda* would manage all digital media for them in future agreements. "I didn't want to discard Facebook entirely in terms of things we want to cover", the CCO said, "because in time we may offer the possibility for brands to have a shopping page directly on Facebook." When Partner Managers first proposed linking e-commerce pages of fashion partners to *Digital Moda*'s own Facebook page, in 2010—thereby conveying the notion of combined value for both parties—they thought deeply about the brand-related consequences of this decision for clients. The idea was to see whether 'fans' of the brand that were also 'fans' of *Digital Moda* on Facebook would be inspired to visit the e-commerce page of the fashion company by clicking on a link from Facebook, and if this kind of aesthetic and commercial "curiosity" traffic would result in a purchase.

The push towards influence legitimacy with existing partners was a delicate matter. First, fledgling e-commerce managers on the other side could be overwhelmed by the changes. Second, the *Partner Division* itself was built in mind with limited marketing competence targeted at fashion partners. The end goal for Partner Managers when employing this vigorous approach with partner brands was to influence e-commerce managers to learn and act quickly on resolving e-commerce challenges in their everyday work. "They need to establish a seamless online reporting structure with us", said the Director of *Partner Division*, proposing that partners undertake further hiring initiatives. "The reporting structure should have an online PR team; a person from their PR department. It could be 2 people—for Facebook and twitter. And at the same time someone in charge of the dialogue with bloggers".

Digital Moda launched the *Partner Division* in mind with transmitting to European and US fashion brands the ability to generate "big, virtual, and imaginary" (US CEO) new ideas online. Given the growing agenda, more roles were added at division level, related to the production and managing of editorial content, e-newsletters, and social media. "The *Partner Division* is becoming its own company", the CCO observed in 2012. Eventually, as its influence legitimacy grew and was challenged, *Digital Moda* took another step in the direction of institutionalizing new competence at a group level. The result was the founding of a new organizational unit, *Pure Brand Unit*.

Extending Pragmatic Legitimacy: Pure Brand Unit

The motivation for establishing *Pure Brand Unit* was to continue affecting the cultural architectures of fashion companies. This latest involvement with changing the culture of established brands was even more significant than what *Digital Moda* had already achieved; managing e-commerce operations for fashion companies. *Digital Moda*'s marketing team aspired to persuade fashion company partners with existing e-commerce operations to leverage new types of partnerships with social commerce peers. The scope of these activities ranged from simple advertising deals with publishers that could be handled in bulk, such as pricing on banner space, to fairly complex and unique initiatives, like running online marketing campaigns for fashion brands and Co-branding. Fashion company partners had to be persuaded to add, on top of the contractually guaranteed SEM work, more complex activities for their fledgling e-commerce teams to handle.

The soft launch of *Pure Brand* was scheduled for mid-2010 and the Global Marketing Director decided to house the team permanently under *Partner Division*. The Director of *Partner Division* identified the role of *Pure Brand Unit* as a "one-stop-shop for *everything digital*" for fashion brands. Consider how this legitimizing narrative differs from Bluefly's slogan in 1996, per which the then-pioneer company strove to become the "one-stop-shop for *fashion*". Given that *Digital Moda* had already established the dimensions of moral and pragmatic legitimacy in the fashion field, it now made sense to extend the reach of legitimacy by influencing organizational structures in fashion companies to cut through established siloes erected between aesthetic and commercial practice. The Director of *Partner Division* hypothesized that for both

parties this was an organic development in leveraging on mutually beneficial practice:

> We would rather leverage on our existing competencies across the organi-
> zation, but for the benefit of fashion partners. We also use the negotiating
> power of *Digital Moda* in order to obtain lucrative or better placements
> with magazines or online publishers for advertising at prices that are a lot
> better for fashion brands. Due to the leveraging power of *Digital Moda*,
> the brand will be better off, instead of trying to [independently] negotiate
> this price.

Another proponent for extending the legitimacy of *Digital Moda* was
the US CEO. He often asserted that fashion companies have locked-
into expensive, impractical, and outdated ways of ensuring aesthetic
exposure to their clients by purchasing print advertising with magazines
(e.g., Vogue). The advent of online marketing rendered this practice
superfluous:

> The reason why we do marketing this way is because it is more cost-ef-
> fective than traditional marketing. First, the conversion rate[1] we get from
> a website form of marketing is much better. It is one thing to be on a
> website, where the product is really *relevant* to this channel. Strategic
> Co-branding [with Social Commerce peers] has also evolved, and become
> a much more *relevant form of marketing*, rather than putting a banner on
> some random website.

Pure Brand would convey to digital teams in fashion partners to curb
their use of a mushrooming number of digital agencies that frequently
tackled identical campaigns on different social media platforms, at different times, and by using diverging slogans. Recall, the dichotomy in
MilanModa1's approach in Chapter 3, where executives with strategic influence founded new structures and practices along established
institutional lines, obfuscating the lack of actual work repertoires.
MilanModa1's Communications division was likewise open to allow
digital agencies handle the production of press content for its Facebook
page, while refusing that this role be performed by an in-house team.

The problem *Digital Moda* was attempting to resolve with the founding of the *Pure Partner Unit* was to facilitate the adoption by fashion
partners of more complex forms of e-commerce, such as online marketing, social media management, and Co-branding. As we learned in

Chapter 3, marketing and communications were under the purview of Communications divisions and were considered to be as proprietary as the function of design in fashion companies. Consequently, communications and PR teams had accustomed to treat Facebook as their personal press release platform. The Global Director of Marketing at *Digital Moda* outlined the difficulty in accomplishing the desired change in partners:

> Social has gotten completely out of our control and is handled by the brands' Press. In an ideal world, there needs to be 360-degree approach. There may be a fashion company that actually does it, if it internalizes the whole process of organizing SEM, online marketing and social media together a part of a unified E-Commerce. But, there is no way for these firms to get a foothold in the digital branding domain independently without our help!

The complex organizational structure of *Digital Moda* expanded with the addition of *Pure Brand* (Fig. 5.4), first imagined as an independent unit located under Group Marketing and managed by the Global Director of Marketing. In order to expedite the testing of new ideas, *Pure Brand* built on overall functional expertise in the company and had four distinct areas of competence in online advertising, fashion editing/style, social media, and coordination of special projects (such as Co-branding). Similar to the multifaceted role of Partner Managers, Editors in *Pure Brand* specialized in more than one functional area of expertise. Their role was explained by the CEO in the US office as a fusion of "[…] more than a copyrighter and more than a stylist, but kind of these both things at the same time. They are really a 'fashion person' who knows how to write." Editors specialized in producing conceptual specials on trend. Style and fashion editors were frequently contracted by

Fig. 5.4 *Pure Brand Unit* (*Source* Internal documents. Simplified organizational structure)

the Commercial Department at group level to perform trend research. The small unit was rounded up by the special projects Coordinator. This expert came up with ideas for developing relationships with fashion partners on projects ranging from Co-branding to capsule collections, in which fashion partners produced fashion product exclusively for *DigitalModa.com* or *Digiluxe.com*.

As is evident, these areas of expertise stretched beyond SEM and into areas distinctly associated with guarded core competence that fashion companies bestowed only to editorial publishers, such as Vogue. The Director of *Pure Brand* attempted to influence e-commerce teams in fashion partner companies that they should push to create consistent work repertoires in e-commerce and not have these spread out across external agencies or divisions:

> Fundamentally, your digital strategy should *not* be one agency doing affiliate, another doing SEM, and another doing social, YouTube videos…. it's a mess. Rather than that, it would be appropriate to say, OK, on the 17th of Sept, we will be launching the new collection. What can we do with that? OK, social, affiliate, SEM, YouTube, twitter. For social we can say, OK, on Facebook we have more fans than in our online store and perhaps we can leverage that to even try to drive traffic to our site. Let's first talk about this event on Facebook, an hour later, let's tweet about it, and 3hrs later, let's send an email to the registered users of the e-site, because the hope is that as the time passes between the one channel and the other, people would have generated traffic to our site and registered themselves to receive email. Ideally, we need a 360-degree servicing and view. This *is* what *Pure Brand* wants to do.

In 2011, at the experimental stage of its development, *Pure Brand* had only three employees across areas of competence and its success depended on the ability of these executives to find distinctive projects for fashion partners. One of the first "special" projects materialized on an impromptu basis when the US CEO observed the runway show of a new fashion label, born in Manhattan's fashion district in 2010. "They're fairly unknown", he said:

> And they wanted to grow their business and become more internationally well known. What can they do? They are a company that makes $5 million a year. They were tiny and they could never take hundred thousand dollars and spend it on a page in Vogue, which is basically what a page in Vogue

costs. What they can do is to sell their fashion collection on *DigitalModa. com*, for $25,000 in this case, and use our global customer base. In this case, we did them a favor, because I kind of like them. Honestly. So, they gave us the product and we gave them the exposure.

With this first special project, the *Pure Brand Unit* commenced to create an array of value-added options for partner brands. The collaboration with this first partner label included an interview with the head designer accessible on the front page of *DigitalModa.com* that led to an e-commerce page, temporarily and exclusively designed for the fashion brand by the *Partner Division* for the duration of the project. The young label was additionally exposed to new audiences by receiving an editorial mention on *DigitalModa.com*. *Digital Moda*, finally, paid for creative photography of fashion product displayed online.

Special Projects were, essentially, brewed as a potent channel that *Digital Moda* could use to communicate its growing fashion authority and influence legitimacy in the field of digital fashion. When working on creating special projects for fashion brands, *Pure Brand*'s first decision was to make sure that there was alignment between the stated goal of the initiative and the desired objectives of the partner. The assessment was intended to ensure that any special project was exclusively tailored to a partner brand. The selling point to existing fashion partners was exposure of known brands to more visibility with new audiences, such as younger audiences visiting *StyleMag* to search for brand promotions, or trafficking *CommunityMag* to create fashion sets. Special Projects also served as an entry point to smaller fashion labels that did not have e-commerce. "They would not even know *who* to contact in the first place", the US CEO plainly explained the appeal of special projects for new brands. "And, if they knew, they would not get the same rates or the same added value."

Another example in the same period, showing the breadth of special project initiatives, was signed between *Digital Moda*'s US office and a well-known US fashion designer. The US CEO and the US Director of Marketing, who both happened to be fervent buyers of the brand, conceived of this collaboration as a local experiment in producing international visibility for the brand and local visibility for *Digital Moda*. The head designer at the US fashion label in question was considered to be "part of the family" in the US office. Collaboration with the label had started in 2004, when the head designer created special jewelry collection for *DigitalModa.com*. The collection had been well received, and the most expensive piece of jewelry had sold for $6000. The relationship with the designer was considered "special" also because one of the former PR Directors at *Digital Moda* became PR Director for this fashion brand in mid-2003.

This collaborative deal included a number of elements. The designer created an exclusive collection featuring t-shirts—a basic item in the fashion industry, but in this case, exclusively designed for *DigitalModa.com*. The capsule t-shirt collection was focused around activism and included a statement against consumerism; representing what the designer considered his own fight for balanced "Social Media and Social Network" era. The designer was responsible only for the logo design of the t-shirts and had requested that his socialite friends model the outfits to be put on the promo webpage on *DigitalModa.com*. The production of this limited edition, however, was done in Italy and *Digital Moda*, not the designer, assumed responsibility for contracting out the production of items. This was also one of the first projects by *Digital Moda* that involved cross-fertilization between social media and brick-and-mortar approach. As with any experiments in practice, the US CEO recalled that there was a learning curve for both partners:

> There were a few things that did not quite work well. First, there was a logistical issue related to lead production times. The samples did not come on time. In fact, only 10–15 samples made it to his friends [who modeled the t-shirts]. The second was a technological preference we had with regard to the Facebook application that we developed to link to the collection. We proposed to make the product, such that it becomes a virtual wearable. However, the designer did not like this idea. This was too bad, because the technological solution was cool.

The project nevertheless ran as a 'special project' accessible to shop via the front page of *DigitalModa.com*. To ensure exclusivity of the proposition, the e-commerce shop was accessible only to registered users of *DigitalModa.com* for six months. The marketing team in the US developed a front-page banner that heralded the arrival of the campaign. The brick-and-mortar part of the event was to introduce the collection by holding a physical event, to which a comprehensive list of designers, models, socialites, and editors were invited. The date coincided with the first day of NYC Fashion Week in 2011. *Digital Moda*'s US office paid a local PR agency for the design and sending out of party invitations.

Publicity costs as well as online campaign costs, as well as costs related to photographing, uploading of the merchandise, and, finally, for newsletter distribution were also covered by *Digital Moda*'s US office.

This special project was designed to be a high-risk event, in spite of the fact that the fashion designer was personally acquainted with *Digital Moda* executives in United States. The US CEO was concerned (unduly, as it turned out) that a relatively small audience would turn out at the physical event (a cocktail party), because cherry-picked invitees could have been invited to a different event for Day 1 of Spring/Summer Fashion Week 2011. In fact, the risk undertaken with executing the event was many times higher than what designers typically preferred to do when promoting new capsule collections—advertise in Vogue. The US CEO directly compared the approaches, "$50,000 is the cost of half a page in Vogue, as a point of comparison. But, it is static. It does nothing for you, commercially and culturally." As with most special projects between *Digital Moda* and fashion partners, the relationship was based on a revenue share. *Digital Moda* was paid a share of sales from the capsule collection.

Within the confines of special projects, *Digital Moda* executives felt secure to experiment with new collaborative practice. Special projects became an exciting new playground, especially in the United States, where fashion companies were less vulnerable than their high-fashion peers in Europe to accept the risk of e-commerce capsule collections or Co-branding. The Special Projects Coordinator kept a log of creative solutions proposed to fashion brands during negotiations. Soon enough, marketing executives in the United States began to obsessively document special project campaigns with fashion brands. By covering some of the creative costs for hosting events, the US office was also taking advantage of the 'culture premium' tactic, aimed at extending pragmatic legitimacy into influence legitimacy with fashion company partners. *Pure Brand Unit* was then, another strategic initiative that ultimately served, as the US CEO explained, as "our first step into the direction of strategic branding with fashion labels and a nice side project that keeps people interested and adds color to [*Digital Moda*]."

INSTITUTIONALIZING INFLUENCE LEGITIMACY: DIGILUXE.COM

During the first ten years of *DigitalModa.com*'s existence, *Digital Moda* gained moral and pragmatic legitimacy in the fashion field. The success of special projects with emerging fashion designers, in particular, convinced US executives that the company, in addition to generating legitimacy with traditional fashion companies, was also popular with new fashion labels and had an easier time communicating the value of influence legitimacy with them, instead of embarking at the start of the social process of legitimation (Johnson et al. 2006).

The executive team in the United States decided to push headquarters in Italy to focus on extending the influence of *Digital Moda* with emerging fashion brands. The result was the formation of a new in-house e-commerce property, *Digiluxe.com*, whose goal would be to acquire product exclusively from emerging fashion brands and run special marketing projects for them. Operationally, *Digiluxe.com* relied on existing skills in the company in merchandising, buying, marketing, and technology. Whereas *DigitalModa.com* was established as a discounted fashion retailer in 2000, ten years later, *Digiluxe.com* was conceived as a full-price e-commerce curating platform for assessing the commercial and aesthetic viability of young designers—in short, nurturing the future of the fashion industry.

The Director of *Digiluxe.com* described the project as *DigitalModa.com*'s "child". A defining characteristic of *Digiluxe.com* was the focus on collaborating with younger fashion companies in producing content. The production of editorial content online, such as video, interviews, photography, curated edits, and Co-branding were a new dimension in *Digital Moda*'s cultural toolset that reflected its growing influence legitimacy with fashion companies. *Digiluxe.com*'s Director explained how the new in-house brand was a marketing catalyst for emerging brands:

> Let's say that *DigitalModa.com* is the place of huge variety of merchandise that is not in the stores at the moment. *Digiluxe.com* is not in competition with all the boutiques out there that may have certain items from the selection. Here we compete on *customized content*. We give every brand featured on *Digiluxe.com* an opportunity to transmit the value of the brand through the content that is built in. In other words, use the Internet to transmit the value of the brand. We also offer an integrated approach in which we have a section for video, etc. and use the Internet technologies to build the brand.

Digiluxe.com was founded only *after Digital Moda*'s executives in the United States, the company's innovation hub, gained expertise and legitimacy for running e-commerce and marketing campaigns on *DigitalModa.com*. *Digiluxe.com* not only represented an evolution in *Digital Moda*'s business competence; it was, more importantly, an exercise in demonstrating influence legitimacy in fashion. New fashion brands had acquired a mentor that introduced them to younger Internet-immersed audiences with the goal of achieving brand loyalty and commercial results. The Director of the *Partner Division* detailed the cultural identity of *Digiluxe.com* as "a more exclusive enclave with niche brands and labels at the higher end of the fashion spectrum." The aesthetic identity of this new experimental hub was thought out as a virtual space that presented "a selection of artisans and cutting-edge brands for men and women with dedicated mini-stores". The US CEO had announced to the fashion industry in the United States that *Digiluxe.com* "is the only place on the Internet where one meets *craft and experimentation*".

The Global Director of Marketing at *Digital Moda* was responsible for creating the 'incubating' narrative around *Digiluxe.com*'s main function. The incubation period concept was defined as the time it took for merchandising and marketing teams at *Digital Moda* in the United States to assess, if young labels had sales potential for an independent e-commerce site. *Digiluxe.com* used the already existing competence of the *Partner Division* in handling special projects, including the ability to sign deals with social commerce partners for powering Co-branding initiatives for young designers. A Brand Director headed *Digiluxe.com*. The Brand Director performed an important role, as she gradually understood that young emerging fashion companies were open to e-commerce to a far greater extent than established European fashion brands. She also realized that while large established fashion companies with well-known brand names had enough critical volume to sustain an e-commerce business, "we decided at that time that there was room for buying in-season merchandise from smaller, younger brands and even niche brands. In these cases, the brand needs to be *supported* in terms of us helping out with the [online] traffic".

The launch of *Digiluxe.com* can be conceptualized as validation of *Digital Moda*'s growing contextual expertise in the field of digital fashion and a further verification for its emerging influence legitimacy. The idea of "helping" brands, obviously, continued as an important narrative in the development of relationships with emerging fashion labels, as it did with established ones. The prime objective of *Digiluxe.com* was to select emerging fashion brands for collaboration. *Digital Moda* had achieved already moral and pragmatic legitimacy around this objective in the fashion field. Furthermore, the founding of the *Partner Division* and the *Pure Brand Unit* had buttressed the ability of the organizational structure to wield these two developed forms of legitimacy. When emerging fashion labels agreed be featured on *Digiluxe.com*, their executive teams were presented with four distinct tiers of collaboration that addressed aesthetic and commercial concerns (Fig. 5.5).

The first 'tier' in the relationship was the creation of a customized e-commerce website for the young partner brand. This was not a stand-alone e-commerce property. Instead, each of the collaborating emerging labels became an "owner" of a shoplet, hosted by and accessible to consumers only via *Digiluxe.com*. Fashion product on these pages was highly curated, in close collaboration with executives on the brand side. Consumers could peruse digital look-books, runways, and special projects with social commerce peers, developed by *Digiluxe.com*'s e-commerce team. The second tier guaranteed to collaborating young labels that *Digital Moda* merchandisers would acquire (buy) a segment of their seasonal collection and curate the acquired inventory on the customized brand e-shop. The partner was guaranteed by contract to a "complete and representative" product curation with the idea to elicit commercial and brand awareness appeal.

Fig. 5.5 Collaboration 'tiers' between *Digiluxe.com* and fashion company partners

To "help" young fashion brands climb out from the vulnerability of the fashion system in the aftermath of the financial crisis was also relatively unproblematic, given the fact that they were, as the Brand Director habitually put it, "cash hungry". *Digital Moda* had already collected a healthy stockpile of established fashion company partners. Young labels were easier to compel at this stage. The process of selecting young and emerging fashion partners was also far simpler. Occasionally, editorial staff in *Digital Moda* US would read an editorial and find a new fashion company, whose look they found fresh and suggest the lead to *Digiluxe. com*'s buyers. At other times, *Digiluxe.com*'s Brand Director herself attended fashion shows. She conveyed enthusiasm and authority about new trends and brands and would directly go for collaboration. "We are very open to include new brands", she clarified during negotiations, "because variety is our value". The Brand Director had constructed a set of persuasive arguments to aspiring, young fashion partners:

> Small brands have a problem that is compounded in economic crises, as retailers try to reduce the inventory from less known brands. Internet is a way to remain in the distribution. [...] When we find a new brand, we try to read, if the right commercial value is there. The right price range, content in terms of wearability, and interest from the press; the brand needs to be a press darling, needs to become a press darling. Together, we can achieve this.

The third tier of collaboration guaranteed young brands aesthetic exposure. Merchandisers would select only a limited number of high-end fashion brands to share online space with the partner during social commerce campaigns or special projects. Part of the selection process was for young brands to actually present data showing they had invested in "innovative or artisanal" production and had limited brick-and-mortar and online distribution. This would then guarantee their eligibility for exposure alongside more established fashion names, when the former became featured in special campaigns. A tiny team at *Digiluxe.com*, consisting of only ten buyers across *Digital Moda*'s offices in Spain, France, Japan, and the USA frequently prepared the selection of merchandise for each of the young brands. This model made it prerequisite for selected brands to have very limited distribution online.

If the young fashion company was "hip, high-fashion and new"; *Digiluxe.com*'s Brand Director argued, but was already featured abundantly either in brick retail or on the e-commerce fronts of other fashion retailers, it was difficult for its executives to be selected. One example was *Digiluxe. com*'s interest in Alexander Wang (at that time, a relatively young American fashion label), whose eponymous designer had launched his first women's collection in 2007. "We are very interested in Alexander Wang", the Brand Director asserted. "[B]ut, he is well spread online right now, which makes it more complicated to put it on *Digiluxe.com*, let's put it this way". These tactics of selection and positioning in the space made it possible for *Digital Moda* to eventually gain exclusive online distribution of young brands, and ability to regulate and control their marketing message.

The fourth tier in the partnership stipulated the "communications" dimension of the collaboration. The experience gained by *Digital Moda* on developing special projects, as part of *Pure Brand*'s mission, permitted *Digiluxe.com* to offer many options for marketing campaigns. Campaigns would be developed together with social commerce partners. In addition, as the influence legitimacy of *Digital Moda* increased, *Digiluxe.com* commenced *advising* emerging fashion companies on how to design their online communications. Producing editorials and curating product in e-newsletters sent out to registered customers, was an initiative staunchly embraced by *Digiluxe.com*. E-newsletters were produced *in collaboration* with young fashion brand partners on *Digiluxe. com*.

One example of imparting, in essence, what was a growing influence legitimacy to young fashion companies was when merchandisers at *Digiluxe.com* selected and placed online runway snapshots for the Japanese street wear fashion label *Undercover*. *Digiluxe.com*'s Brand Director explained to executives from the brand the importance of this exposure: "This is a mix between product and content. Both journalists and customers find content for their use at these projects. We organized snapshots of video from the catwalk online and curated wearable and potentially highly sellable, but unique product. Next year, we plan [to do] the same for Jil Sander for women and Aider Ackerman for men, for example." Eventually, other contemporary fashion brands, such as Alexander Wang, joined the roster of young fashion brands with e-commerce exposure on *Digiluxe.com*. The option for customers to engage interactively with viewing the content of runway shows from these contemporary high-fashion brands expanded over time, from "Watching the Runway show now" to "Reserving Your Look now" and buying upcoming products from the runway.

The Brand Director at *Digiluxe.com* candidly revealed that the development of overall legitimacy at *Digital Moda* over the years would not have been possible without its first e-commerce brand, *DigitalModa. com*. The cultural heritage of *DigitalModa.com* was kept animated throughout the development of competence and legitimacy in the company. *Digiluxe.com* had to pay homage to this origin of legitimacy by featuring special projects and capsule collections from young labels on *DigitalModa.com*. "From our customer perspective", the Brand Director pointed out, "we know that the value that the final customer sees in [*DigitalModa.com*] is the variety of brands—from very large to very niche brands. It's a kind of a 'bible', our 'bible' of so many brands, and we know that our customers recognize us for this."

NOTE

1. Conversion rate is measured by the share of visitors to a website that take a desired action by the e-commerce team. This action could be signing up for an e-newsletter, registering with an account with a login and password, purchasing, or something else.

BIBLIOGRAPHY

Deephouse, D.L., & Suchman, M. (2008). Legitimacy in organizational institutionalism. In Greenwood, R., Oliver C., Suddaby R., & Sahlin-Andersson K. (Eds.), *The Sage handbook of organizational institutionalism* (49–77). London: Sage.

Johnson, C., Dowd, T.J., & Ridgeway, C.L. (2006). Legitimacy as a social process. *Annual Review of Sociology, 32,* 53–78.

Meyer, J.W., & Rowan, B. (1977). Institutionalized organizations: Formal structure as myth and ceremony. *American Journal of Sociology, 83*(2), 340–363.

Scardaville, M.C. (2009). High art, no art: The economic & aesthetic legitimacy of US soap operas. *Poetics, 37*(4), 366–382.

Suchman, M. (1995). Managing legitimacy, strategic & institutional approaches. *Academy of Management Review, 20*(3), 571–610.

CHAPTER 6

The Fruits of "Creative Disruption": Influence Legitimacy and Tech Culture Transfer to Fashion Industry Gatekeepers

As we established in Chapter 2, *Digital Moda* had a pioneering involvement with firing up collaborative agreements with social commerce companies, right after these new players arrived around 2006 into the emerging arena of digital fashion. The goal of peer collaboration, although immediately related to helping these partners gain institutional legitimacy in the field of fashion, eventually became to leverage existing partnerships with social commerce players in the direction of achieving an existential milestone in the fashion industry; namely, to blur the existing institutional boundaries separating the work of brick-and-mortar fashion publishers (long the magisterial domain of fashion magazines, like Vogue) and fashion retail (contemporaneously administered by large department stores). Achieving influence legitimacy of this kind would be a genuine challenge to the industry 'proper' and the crux in commanding *Digital Moda*'s legitimacy in the industry. Even though by 2011, *Digital Moda* had succeeded in reaching noteworthy strides in moral and pragmatic legitimacy in the field, fashion brands were still unwilling to engage social commerce companies in their endorsement process. The Global Marketing Director noted the extreme moral apprehension of fashion companies in this way:

> Fashion brands are not exposed to this form of collaboration because they *hate* [Social Commerce] publishers. As a partner, my perception is that some of our brands are forward thinking and they are not afraid to take radical steps [...] brands like these, which have this built into their culture,

it would be very easy to work with them and for them to be receptive to these ideas.

Thus, on the way to earning influence legitimacy in the institutional field of fashion, *Digital Moda* needed to succeed in persuading fashion partners that its peers in social commerce were legitimate collaborators in the new field (Powell 2012). The company would achieve this by manipulating its existing position with fashion company partners and exploiting "contradictions embedded in dominant institutional logics" (Suddaby and Greenwood 2005, p. 36) in the brick-and-mortar field, rather than—as we have well established by now—by "conform[ing] to [the existing] environments" (Suchman 1995, p. 587) and obeying prevailing relations between fashion magazines, retailers, and fashion companies.

To confront this problem of conferring peer-level legitimacy in the field, the Marketing Director at the US office decided that *Digital Moda*'s team would select only social commerce partners that the marketing team had previously cleared as "appropriate" for luxury fashion exposure. In this sense, "appropriate" meant that an affiliate partner was not evaluated merely on the basis of their ability to generate sales, but additionally, on the proficiency of its editors in writing well-informed fashion editorials during promotional campaigns. Partnership agreements with social commerce companies, other than *Digital Moda*'s largest partners *StyleMag* and *CommunityMag*, were mediated by one of the largest affiliate marketing service providers online, Rakuten LinkShare. This online platform was a marketing mediator that introduced *Digital Moda* to a large prospective pool of social commerce publishers, ranging from well-known online magazines to niche fashion bloggers.

Digital Moda was a premium account holder at LinkShare. Two Account Managers, one Creative Services specialist, an analyst, and a legal team from LinkShare handled affiliate relationships for *Digital Moda*. Through LinkShare, the marketing team in the US office had instant access to a representative sample of Internet's most recognized, commercially successful social commerce publishers. This type of disclosure was available *only* to e-commerce peers holding "premium account" status. The US CEO explained that the legitimacy of LinkShare as the largest marketing service platform online had a way of persuading fashion partners in accepting collaboration with social commerce publishers. "In order to converse about your expertize with fashion partners", he said, "you have to use the help of someone who *has authority in many different fields*".

LinkShare picked up an account management fee for its mediating role and provided *Digital Moda*'s marketing team in the US with weekly analysis of performance for its marketing affiliates. As a premium account holder, *Digital Moda* had access to more than a thousand affiliate partners. Each of these affiliates received access to banners, text links, and curated product, and used these assets in campaign promotions for *Digital Moda*. This type of mass access of many publisher affiliates to several marketing campaign assets was called "public" affiliation. Holding premium account status, however, also had "private affiliation" advantages for *Digital Moda*. Private affiliation meant that instead of permitting a slew of smaller publishers to benefit from participating in a promotional campaign, LinkShare, instead, invited only "the cream of the crop" of social commerce, such as *StyleMag*. This form of partner segmentation was used when the marketing team at *Digital Moda* in the US sought to demonstrate that it was up to them to share their exclusive access to fashion company partners with only select few social commerce associates.

Account managers at LinkShare and the marketing team in the US office frequently held face-to-face dialogs, in which *Digital Moda*'s executives unfailingly communicated their key position in the emerging field of digital fashion and their growing influence legitimacy in the fashion industry. The Director of Marketing in the US frequently reiterated to account managers at LinkShare, that "as you know, we are a luxury brand and we'd like to keep an eye on how we're presented in each channel". Marketing team members also regularly went over *Digital Moda*'s e-commerce expertise. "We are finalizing our promotional engine", explained one US marketing executive to LinkShare's account team. "The idea of the promotional engine is to come up with a list of promotions that we could tailor to each of our affiliates. For [a fashion partner] for example, this would be a great conversation. How do we boost their ROI (return on investment) by promotions, given that they are available in so many other merchants?"

Owing to this premium account status, marketing executives at *Digital Moda* enjoyed the privilege of holding informal discussions with the executive teams of potential social commerce partners before including these into their existing network of affiliates. The goal here was to persuade the other side in disclosing key aspects of their own narratives for legitimization with fashion companies. This discussion was informal but consistently centered on two areas of discourse: cultural and

Table 6.1   Ensuring alignment in collaborating with social commerce partners

Cultural goals	Commercial goals
Why did you start the business and what do you expect to achieve from it?	What makes you profitable and unique—technology, community?
Why would consumers visit you and not any other publishers?	What is your revenue model?
What campaigns would you use to attract established or new fashion companies?	

commercial (Table 6.1). By directing several exploratory questions from each of these two areas, marketing executives at *Digital Moda* made sure that potential partners understood the value of cultural alignment.

"Only after establishing these questions can I ask more *quantitative stuff* such as revenue, unique visitors, community members, conversion rates", observed the US Marketing Director. A prospective affiliate had a chance of being included as "brand-appropriate", if they employed a creative approach to publishing that included multiple revenue streams from curation of fashion editorials; blog and community activity; technical agility; and, the ability to create value-added services, such as brand contests (Chapter 2).

MilanModa3, one of *Digital Moda*'s first e-commerce fashion company partners, similarly, became the first to try social commerce exposure. *Digital Moda* benefited from this significant decision by an established fashion company by becoming the first e-commerce player to create an exclusive "private" social commerce project. Part of the enticement of private affiliation was to present to strategic executives in *MilanModa3* that there were advantages in being an insider to "brand-appropriate" partners in the digital ecology of fashion. The hook was that *MilanModa3* could not have negotiated the same (significantly lower) account management fee for private affiliation that included multiple, high-end social commerce partners. The advantage of having many fashion brand partners, correspondingly, allowed *Digital Moda* to convince account executives at its marketing service provider to agree on charging the same fee for three further European fashion clients.

The list of affiliated social commerce peers in this exclusive "private" program for *MilanModa3* included some 50 "brand-appropriate" channels. This number was not inadvertent. Only around 15% of these affiliates were expected to generate sales for *MilanModa3*'s campaign.

The idea was to diversify the exposure to risk associated with the commercial performance of affiliates by letting in few extra affiliates for prominence of status. *Digital Moda*'s US marketing team decided that a combination of esthetic and commercial goals would be appropriate for this first partnership. With this decision, *Digital Moda*'s Marketing Director in the US hoped to set a standard that exposed *MilanModa3* to accepting that social commerce partnerships generated not only commercial but furthermore esthetic—brand and awareness-related—value. During the first year of the affiliate program for *MilanModa3* in 2011, the commercial results generated by the select fifty social commerce partners exceeded $10 million. This was considered to be a significant commercial and brand exposure for *MilanModa3*, given the small size of the affiliate partner sample in the experiment. The results during this test-drive year of private affiliation received positive endorsement from the US-based e-commerce manager at *MilanModa3*'s office in New York, and at Milan headquarters, where executives agreed that the brand would continue investing in private affiliation.

DISSIMILAR CULTURES, DIVERGENT RESULTS: BRICK-AND-MORTAR MEDIA PUBLISHERS AND PRAGMATIC LEGITIMACY

On a morning in February 2011, a lively discussion started between the Head of Merchandising, the Director of Marketing and the CEO at *Digital Moda*'s office in NYC. The team had to consider the impact of new developments in the digital field of fashion, in which established media conglomerates acquired social commerce fashion companies. On January 19th 2010, *Time Inc.* had announced that InStyle.com, one of its largest fashion magazines online, had acquired StyleFeeder.com, a social commerce company that enabled users to browse the web and add a variety of merchandise, including fashion product, to a personalized 'StyleFeed', which they could then share with friends. Time Inc. had disclosed that the acquisition went forward because StyleFeeder.com had designed an improved search algorithm that analyzed the 'StyleFeeds' of users and came up with relevant product recommendations. In November 2010, using the new pattern recognition technology, Time Inc. rebranded StyleFeeder.com into a stand-alone social commerce Website, called StyleFind.com.

The development was important to the three abovementioned executives at *Digital Moda*, because StyleFind.com was conceived as a social commerce Website with identical competence to that of *StyleMag* and *CommunityMag*. The site featured an edited daily selection of top fashion trends, "editor's picks" spotlighting desired fashion pieces, and a "deals section" that highlighted daily sales across a number of e-commerce retailers. *Digital Moda*'s executives were concerned that StyleFind.com would eventually "power shopping on InStyle.com". This was going to cause disruption in the digital field of fashion. InStyle was an influential fashion media magazine and had direct advertising relationships with fashion companies. A successful integration between StyleFind.com and InStyle.com would mean that a significant portion of fashion companies' advertising budgets might go to the digital wing of InStyle. The US executives pondered if the culture of a social commerce start-up, as StyleFind, could actually be aligned with that of a traditional fashion media magazine, like InStyle.

The Marketing Director asserted that in comparison with long-term partners of *Digital Moda*, like *StyleMag*, curation and editorial choices on StyleFind.com were "over-curated". What this observation meant, was that the selected fashion styles, lifestyle ideas, and brands on StyleFind.com were excessively and cautiously curated to appeal to only a specific clientele online. The US CEO proclaimed that this was a "cultural legacy" inherited from InStyle.com, the parent fashion publishing company. The conversation had turned into a social scientist's daydream: a direct comparison between "thinking" and "doing" in new versus established companies in the field, where executives representing new, innovative models predicted that traditional fashion media gatekeepers would fail to understand how to transition their thinking and behavior online.

As per the Head of Merchandising, the thinking of executives at InStyle.com had been "schooled around curation—one of the basic and most fundamental functions of a publication—rather than creating awareness for the *content* that it curates". The US CEO pointed out that *StyleMag* and *CommunityMag* had a more "democratized" approach to curation, in which retailers and consumers discovered each other by trusting that merchandisers and fashion editors at *StyleMag* would match their editorial picks with desired consumer product. InStyle.com's philosophy, the US CEO thought, was to first, have online editors select only certain, preferred fashion labels with which InStyle had an ongoing advertising relationship and only then rely on a search and recommendation system that directed the user to these very preferential products and brands. This behavior contradicted fundamental principles by which e-commerce and social commerce fashion entrepreneurs abided, such as the principle of democratizing 'curation' for the consumer. Since their first collaboration with *StyleMag*, the marketing team at *Digital Moda* had scrupulously documented results from collaborating with social commerce peers. Beginning with the desire for their own brand (*DigitalModa.com*) and their partner brands to be found, the quest for partnering with social commerce peers in the emergent space was always focused on enabling each other's reach. For *Digital Moda*, the desired reach was to potential customers; for partners like *StyleMag*, the idea was gaining exposure with fashion brands. The Marketing Director recounted this beneficial collaboration dynamic:

> For multi-brand retailers, like us... it is like a food chain. If you are searching for *Digital Moda*, you can find it in two ways: one, you search for a brand; or two, you search for *Digital Moda*. Google's algorithm has become more complex, with intelligent crawlers; you have relevance that comes into play. And, once you've seen the actual offering you have been looking for... then, the question of credibility and dialogue starts. So, your [Social Commerce] affiliates now have to say: *Digital Moda - your number one source for fashion!* ...It is a continuous improvement. It is an evolution. It is a relationship between fashion brands and us.

The Head of Merchandising explained that the striking contrast between *StyleMag* and StyleFind's curating approach originated in their preference for dissimilar practices, reinforced by the conflicting cultures of the two organizations:

> *StyleMag* is more social plus shopping. So, there is social, there is content, and there is shopping (product). The "holy trinity" of digital branding, I might add. But, if we go to StyleFind, it has an element of pure editorial, where fashion editors say; 'these are the bags of 2011'. They, for example, talk about chunky platforms and then they say, "shop all", and would have the editors pick "all". I remember, when StyleFind was launching, they were supposed to have 50 per cent product and 50 per cent content.

Social commerce pioneers based their editorial role on the idea of combining commercial reach with esthetic value for themselves, their partners, and the final customer. Over time, this cultural goal resulted in new practices, such as product editorials for e-commerce fashion retailers in order to increase their own esthetic exposure as a legitimate partner for fashion brands. Peers in social commerce expected StyleFind.com to approach and legitimize its practice analogously to them. Instead, the new member of the ecology in the digital field of fashion focused on driving revenue through product exclusivity.

Predictably, StyleFind.com did not drive fashion product from e-commerce companies, like *Digital Moda* or *Luxemod*. Instead, its editors displayed curated content from traditional brick-and-mortar retailers, like Nordstrom, Saks 5th Av., and Kmart. "Curating content to the max, such as presenting expensive merchandise from individual brands that happen to be this or that blogger's favorite", exclaimed the Head of Merchandising, "is unlikely to drive revenue, unless the shopping site that is supposed to sell this curated content also happens to be a well-known brand". In the thus outlined brainstorming session, the three executives at *Digital Moda* projected that without alignment with existing Co-branding practice developed between social commerce and e-commerce companies in the digital field of fashion, StyleFind would fail to attract unique audiences.

This collective prediction was confirmed. In the remaining year before Time Inc. folded StyleFind.com's operations, most of the traffic to the Website originated from fashion readers of its parent media magazines, InStyle.com and People.com, the two largest Time Inc. publications online. The curator site attracted 722,000 unique visitors in December 2010 and a slightly smaller population of 498,000 in September 2011. These numbers were but a modest representation of InStyle's own visitor traffic, which only for December 2011 had 6.33 million visitors (Rank2traffic.com, 2017). Ultimately, StyleFind's extraordinary reliance on the daily curation decisions of InStyle fashion editors reduced the likelihood that StyleFind.com would seek Co-branding relationships with e-commerce companies. The lack of sustained rapport with other companies in the digital field of fashion minimized the exposure of this emerging actor to new fashion audiences and practice. Online, relationships between collaborating parties—e-commerce and social commerce, and fashion companies—were just as important, as those nurtured in traditional media, communications, and retail. *StyleMag*'s online editors, for example, frequently "checked in" with *Digital Moda*'s marketing team in New York to see what editorial picks across *Digital Moda*'s properties (*DigitalModa.com*; *Digiluxe.com*) and fashion company partners, have surfaced as "hot" during the week. Consequently, *StyleMag* would feature some of these styles and fashion brands on its editorials.

Occasionally, StyleFind's editors would send generic emails to the Director of Marketing in the US office, asking if he would agree that a product or a fashion brand from any of *Digital Moda*'s online properties or partner e-commerce Websites, could be featured as an "editorial pick of the week". *Digital Moda*'s Marketing Director contemplated that without any underlying conversation regarding *Digital Moda*'s curation techniques or Co-branding partnerships, StyleFind's longevity in the digital space of fashion would be limited:

> They [StyleFind.com] can promote whatever product they want. This is at [*Luxemod*]; this is at DKNY. When we click on this dress, this shows us the link to the page. This is a fairly decent model, because they are using the product listing from [*Luxemod*], DKNY, or from [*DigitalModa.com*], and they are choosing the products and displaying them. But, again, I don't think that [*Luxemod's*] editors or merchandisers had anything to do with the selection, because our products, for example, have been chosen by their editor's picks quite a few times. I just get an email saying: 'hi, how are you? We'd like to publish this product on our website as an editor's pick'.

The lack of direct contact between editors at StyleFind and large brand-promoters, like *Digital Moda*, presented InStyle.com's newest 'sister' business with an organizational deficiency, that presented major technical challenge. Because StyleFind's editors did not ascertain how "hot" the fashion merchandise they linked to would be, StyleFind's customers frequently encountered a "sold out" message at the other side of an editorially recommended link. "If the editor would have called us", said the Head of Merchandising at *Digital Moda*, "we would have said that the product is out of stock, or whatever". Executives at *Digital Moda* reflected on this frequent lack of product availability as a factor that limited potential revenue streams for StyleFind, but also contributed to a crisis of legitimacy for the established fashion owner, InStyle.com. *Digital Moda*'s Marketing Director insisted that, if StyleFind.com pursued an ongoing revenue-share agreement with *Digital Moda*, its crisis of legitimacy would be averted. *Digital Moda*'s technology predicted if a fashion item became scarce ("sold out") and suggested other similar fashion styles instead. "What you see here", the executive said, is a classic example of one person trying to do everything in an *authoritarian way*! The editor has put together the product, has written the content, maybe the designer has put together the page, but there is no interaction between her and the merchant [e.g., *Digital Moda*]. If she would have picked up the phone and said, 'hey, I want to choose this product or something'. That obviously is going to be a pain in the ass; every day, if you want to change the look on the website can be a problem, because you will have to talk to the actual retailer. We know our products really well. You power the content and we power the product.

Fashion media publishers that transferred their brick-and-mortar perspective of "authoritarian" curation to the Internet were not successful, because of a very simple reason: they did not speak with their digital peers or existing fashion companies with e-commerce properties online. As a result, this behavior of avoidance by StyleFind, based on its parent company' perceived authority in the fashion industry, had undesirable implications to the business. In this case study, StyleFind sought to benefit from its pragmatic legitimacy in fashion, but stumbled due to low moral legitimacy in the field of digital fashion. *Digital Moda*'s marketing team, conversely, saw the technical opportunities that seamlessly integrated product and content online as favorable to experimenting with other peers in building legitimacy with fashion companies. Doing it alone, as the US CEO concluded, was "not in the DNA" of e-commerce and social commerce peers inhabiting the field of digital fashion.

Similar Cultures, Divergent Results: Google Ventures and Moral Legitimacy

Similar to brick-and-mortar fashion publishers, Internet pioneers with core businesses outside of fashion were not impervious to failure. In this case study, Google sought to benefit from its moral legitimacy in technology, but stumbled, due to relatively low pragmatic legitimacy in the fashion field. In 2011, Google Inc., the world's largest search engine, announced that it was launching a new social commerce company, Boutiques.com. Apparel had been the fastest growing segment in digital commerce for the three preceding years, and Google was not resistant to diversifying revenue streams and exploring latest commercial technology. Boutiques.com was founded as a fashion search engine and was perceived by the then-team members to be a "personalized *visual* fashion-shopping engine". This self-identification stemmed from the technology of visual search on the basis of which Boutiques.com was founded. Google launched the start-up in November 2010, after acquiring Like.com in August 2010. Like.com was a visual search engine, founded in 2006, after years of efforts by its parent company Riya to monetize technologies of facial search recognition. Prior to the acquisition by Google, Like.com had already experimented with curation by acquiring, opening, and unfortunately, folding the shopping personalization engine Covet.com; the street style social network Weardrobe; and, the visual styling tool Couturious.

The CEOs of *StyleMag* and *CommunityMag*—competitors to Google's new venture—surmised that Google wished to extend its search engine business into a social commerce business, thereby becoming "the starting point where people look for fashion". The acquisition allowed Google, *Digital Moda*'s Marketing Director surmised, to redistribute natural search traffic related to fashion away from social commerce players and into Boutiques.com, thereby claiming legitimacy as a curator and editor in online fashion. The Director of Marketing further theorized that Boutiques.com was launched as an *experiment*. He asserted that the launch was done not for commercial diversification on part of the parent group, but for "checking in" with the rest of existing e-commerce and social commerce players in digital fashion:

> Fashion is going to be decimal point of what the total turnover of Google is, simply because there is only so much volume that you could drive through women's fashion. But, what Google.com is for search, they want to make Boutiques.com for fashion. Once you search over there, you can shop by designers, bloggers' favorite items. In fact, we [*Digital Moda*] are now trying to put more brands onto Boutiques.com, because knowing that this is Google, it will become popular very, very soon.

Fundamentally, Boutiques.com was founded on principles of collaboration with existing e-commerce players, and this ran contrary to the kind of autonomous curation objectives that StyleFind's executives had when launching their venture. While StyleFind was created to legitimate a new slice in Time Inc.'s involvement in Internet-based ventures, Boutiques.com was an experiment in augmenting the pragmatic legitimacy of the parent company, Google, as an innovator in search technology into the domain of digital fashion. Business development executives at Boutiques.

com quickly established contracts with e-commerce retailers and a set of qualitative criteria in approaching them. True to its data collection culture, the Boutiques.com team was aggressive about signing in partners with access to top-dollar fashion brands and quick to develop a qualitative scale on which *Digital Moda* scored 9 out of 10 points as a product share partner. A former executive at the venture called this

> *a retailer screening process.* It is quite qualitative, actually. As a department store may or may not feature certain brands, we have a team of editors, fashion editors, if you will, who decide what retailer we should feature. They have very fashionable product and they carry a lot of it. We would like to have certain products that these affiliates have.

Boutiques.com was important to the online ecology in digital fashion. Due to the scope of its operations, success or failure was going to have ramifications to the entire community in e-commerce fashion. In fact, when Google decided to fold the venture after six months, the Director of Marketing at *Digital Moda* was unenthusiastic about the long-term effects of the closure. "The demise of Boutiques.com", he offered, "will lead to lower overall commissions to affiliates, but also to lower sales".

Six months past the dismantling of the start-up, the marketing team at *Digital Moda* assembled to reflect on the reasons for the fold of Boutiques.com. Contrary to their conclusion regarding StyleFind's demise, the New York team did not believe that the closing of Boutiques.com was a failure on Google's part. The earlier assumption by the Director of Marketing that this was an experiment still held and was bolstered by what Google subsequently did. For now, it suffices to say that the Director of Marketing immediately reasoned that Google would—likely and soon—envision testing new avenues for improving the core area of competence—*search*. "A browser, a search engine, and an operating system – this is what Google is", he said. "It is not a fashion search engine or a premium content aggregator. It is, simply, the three things above. And, whatever they create or build to mimic the fancy social media fad of the moment, they will ultimately use it to improve the areas that they are most competent on".

The opening and successive closure of Boutiques.com had a wide-ranging impact on e-commerce and social commerce companies in digital fashion. It was *Google*, after all, that had decided to venture in and briskly, venture out of digital fashion. The development prompted merchants and publishers, like *Digital Moda* and *StyleMag*, to search for gray areas in the practice of the late start-up that had precipitated its demise. The Head of Merchandising in the US office thought that Boutiques.com had "inconsistency of designer presentation". For example, Boutiques.com had three separate parts on its Website devoted to designers. One was a niche content featuring "Designers"; the second was a niche devoted to "Designer Boutiques"; and, the third part consisted of items "Inspired" by luxury fashion designers and brands.

Some parts of this segmentation, such as the alphabetical list of featured designers highlighted in the "Designers" area, were problematic. Unlike merchants, like *Digital Moda*, Boutiques.com did not have direct relationships with fashion companies, or authorization from such to feature their name in addition to linking to their product. Business development staff at Boutiques.com had not asked for consent from e-commerce fashion merchants for this creative deriving of a list of "designers". This fact ostensibly provoked Digital Moda to consider the question for rightful representation of fashion partners. Finally, the "Inspired by Brand X" section of the Website consisted of fashion products that were "handpicked", as per one executive, by Boutiques' editors. The logic of curation here depended on the tastes of merchandisers at Boutiques, who could predict well how fast certain fashion items would sell. Upon triggering the mouse over a product from any 'inspirational' brand, the customer was presented with a list of fashion apparel from different brands that were determined to be similar in quality, price, and design. Frequently, however, these 'similar' brands put to user's attention were at much lower price points. The lack of awareness by Boutiques.com for the institutional importance of price revealed the main problem with this approach—Boutiques.com lacked moral legitimacy in fashion.

The problem, as *Digital Moda*'s NYC team saw it, was twofold and both reasons had to do with a shortage of moral legitimacy in the fashion industry. First, *Digital Moda* had understood that a significant part of their moral legitimacy-building with fashion companies depended on asking a brand for permission each time that its fashion product was to be listed with other, similar brands on any of *Digital Moda*'s e-commerce properties (Fig. 5.5). Second, even if a luxury brand were to be handpicked for the "Inspired by" section, it was not always clear (absent direct communication with company's merchandisers) if that fashion brand desired to be listed as "inspirational" to other brands. While the "inspired" aspect of this curation method was "democratizing" the representation and access of customers to newer, smaller, or cheaper fashion brands, the three separate "Designer" parts of Boutiques.com's Website were aimed at bypassing negotiations with fashion brands and e-commerce retailers like *Digital Moda* that had exclusive online distribution with them. *Digital Moda* had been successful, in part, because the company understood the tacit rules of moral legitimation in the fashion industry and adapted them to the online domain. Without legitimacy, technology was unlikely to be successful.

"The unique value proposition for the digital publishing industry today", the Marketing Director in the US explained, "comes from making choices *for* customers, merchants, *and for fashion brands*, easier and more relevant based on curation". Even though the technology of price comparison search is what enabled the model of social commerce to gain traction in digital fashion, it was the social commitment to negotiating with fashion brands and liaising with their merchandisers on selecting fashion content, that propelled these organizations to succeed in the long run.

Shortly after the demise of Boutiques.com, Burak Gokturk, co-founder of Like.com, reflected on the *Google Commerce Blog* (2011) that the main goal of Boutiques was to enhance the shopping experience on Google Shopping, a Google service, which allowed users to search for products on e-commerce Websites and compare prices between different vendors. Like.com's team eventually proceeded to incorporate visual search features into Google Product Search "to inspire and facilitate easy, enjoyable browsing and shopping. As we continue to integrate technology and lessons learned from Boutiques.com into Google Product Search", Gokturk explained in 2011, "we will be redirecting shoppers from Boutiques.com to Google Product Search. The former Like.com team, alongside the Google Product Search team, will drive new ideas for apparel shopping through one unified product".

Prescient about the future, a few months before Boutiques.com folded, the Marketing Director in *Digital Moda*'s New York office decided to help out launch a project with a startup entrepreneur, whom he thought, "is proposing to do what Boutiques.com should have been". The budding entrepreneur had sourced 30 well-known e-commerce fashion retailers and 10 individual fashion designers to personally curate their individual webpages on a collaborative basis. Even though the idea would not be easily scaled up, the deduction is that achieving moral legitimacy is the first step in the lifecycle of collaboration between e-commerce, social commerce, and fashion companies.

"The 2.0 Stuff[1]": Co-branding and the Culture Premium

During the early months of 2011, a designated team at Digital Moda's US office, consisting of the Director of Marketing, the Coordinator of Special Projects, the Head of Merchandising, and the CEO, initiated a search for new partnership ideas with social commerce publishers. *Digital Moda* was about to expand direction as *"the global internet company* for the leading fashion and design brands" (Global Director of Marketing) and the US office decided to position its team at the forefront of initiatives that would graduate the company from spending only the technical portion of its clients' digital budgets for SEM activities and keywords to coordinating the entire online marketing budget of their partners. An idea had emerged during meetings with social commerce publishers—any new partnerships between *Digital Moda* and publishers had to include new types of practice for fashion partners that would be "more integrated", feature additional marketing and promotional activities, and encompass a longer duration, from 6 months to over 1 year. *Digital Moda*'s US Director of Marketing hypothesized that following the strengthening of new practices with social commerce publishers, traditional magazine publishers in the fashion industry, such as Vogue, would open up for similar collaboration.

As a recap, *Digital Moda* launched Co-branding as an emergent practice in digital fashion between 2010 and 2012. Co-branding was introduced to *Digital Moda* headquarters in Milan in 2010, coinciding with the launch of *Pure Brand Unit*. Co-branding campaigns for fashion partners would be designed and implemented only with social commerce partners that were "brand-appropriate" and built on the *complementary* skills of partners in product and content curation. "Our unique proposition is the following", said the Special Projects Coordinator at *Pure Brand Unit*. "You have great *content*, but we have a great *product*. The successful idea is to match both". The Coordinator defined Co-branding as a distributed social practice in which

> A product [is] integrated editorially with a shopping area that becomes a *dedicated space* with products powered by *DigitalModa.com*. It is usually a section that is editorially curated. The partnership always involves an editorial component. We usually try to involve the editors of the magazine or community. This would be anyone involved in fashion content or lifestyle content on this magazine or site to collaborate with us.

The role of social commerce partners was to serve as curators in the collaboration. *Digital Moda* created the shopping and product experience: a dedicated e-commerce webpage on which editorial content and fashion product would be integrated for the duration of the campaign. Editors from the publisher's side also crafted the fashion theme around which the curation campaign was developed. Merchandisers from *Digital Moda* chose the fashion product, style, and brand to which the campaign would link. Each Co-branding relationship was designed to be singularly specific to individual social commerce and fashion company partners. The curated shopping page—called "Co-branding page"—showcased the visual strengths of each partner.

Co-branding was a departure from traditional affiliation programs. It introduced a non-commercial, editorial component to a conventionally commercial relationship where one partner, a social commerce company, promoted a brand or a product from another partner, e-commerce fashion retailer. "Affiliation worked as revenue-share", the Special Projects Coordinator explained the difference between earlier forms of affiliated programs and Co-branding,

> But, the minute the fashion editors in *CommunityMag* or *StyleMag* decide to create a customized page picking products from us, this is already in-between affiliation and Co-branding. Co-branding partnerships create a situation in which there is an exchange of visibility between *DigitalModa.com* or any of our client stores and the [Social Commerce] partner. We decided to create this dedicated page hosted on the partner's website. This is a way to get awareness from the readers. We also give visibility to this partner on *DigitalModa.com*.

Hence, the chosen conceptual designation by partners was 'Co-branding'. As we noted, one of the inherent challenges of Co-branding was the continued mistrust of fashion partners vis-à-vis social commerce peers. Even though by 2012 *Digital Moda*'s fashion partners were moving more investment into the digital channel, newly founded e-commerce teams in these—helped by *Digital Moda*'s Partner Division and *Pure Brand*—had to continually justify to executive panels across their organizations that they were taking on an expanding menu of esthetic and commercial opportunities in e-commerce.

"We *do* hold our clients' ad money", the US CEO argued, "[w]hat we would like [is] to play an even more significant role in the budget. Most of this goes to technical channels, like SEM, but we can push through consulting role into other channels". In order to persuade partners to take on longer-term Co-branding agreements with social commerce allies, the US team called *Pure Brand* to action. Through consulting, the unit had to generate sustained interest in Co-branding from partners. Earlier in the discovery process of Co-branding, in 2010, one of the oldest Italian luxury fashion company partners of *Digital Moda* requested more information about the nature of the practice. It was difficult for partners to shift gears and reflect on social commerce companies as an important new social group in digital fashion publishing, quite distinct from established magazines in the industry. After a series of short conversations with that fashion partner "the insight was lost", as one *Digital Moda* executive put it. *Pure Brand* next approached two fashion companies that had been first in launching e-commerce with *Digital Moda* since 2006. To get their consent to linking curated product from their e-commerce Website onto an external social commerce partner page took long hours of teleconferencing between merchandisers in New York, *Pure Brand* Special Project Coordinator in Milan and the e-commerce team on the other side. The substance of these conversations focused on extending influence legitimacy at *Digital Moda* into influence in the areas of communications and publishing online. The approach was tested firstly, in the two fashion company partners, and owing to its successful implementation, became part of *Digital Moda*'s package of practice aimed at acquiring influence legitimacy with fashion companies.

As an increasing number of *Digital Moda*'s fashion partners became open to social commerce campaigns, the company augmented the scope of its Co-branding partnerships with social commerce players. *StyleMag* and *CommunityMag*—the largest partners in the field—were no longer exclusive collaborators. Other smaller, niche, and fashion-forward new publishers, such as *Tablet Magazine, BlackBook Magazine, PaperMag*, and *GenArt*, entered the fold. The US marketing team launched campaigns with smaller publishers as experiments "on a very, very small scale and with little money" as one executive put it. "We pick up four themes from the publisher; no more, and this is how we ensure to stay selective for our fashion partners", said the Special Projects Coordinator. "They send us the four looks. They then ask us: 'can you curate a look, whereby you pick from your designer collection pieces that complete and most closely correspond to this palette and link it with E-Commerce for people to shop?'"

As an increasing number of fashion partners evaluated social commerce partnerships positively, merchandising teams at fashion companies insisted to participate, and indeed, weigh-in on the value of proposed social commerce campaigns. This was an affirmative development. In the course of cultivating *Digital Moda*'s influence legitimacy, *Pure Brand Unit* developed additional steps in the collaborative process to ensure that new e-commerce units at fashion partners were becoming infused with tech culture. In advance to signing a deal, *Digital Moda*'s marketing team at the *Partner Division* hurried to equip e-commerce partner teams with decision-making power on their e-commerce Website in curating the appropriate styles that they thought corresponded to an editorial fashion "look" desired by a social commerce partner. Having the input from fashion companies was a vital prerequisite for the success of Co-branding campaigns with smaller publishers, because fewer styles calibrated the browsing behavior of customers, introducing them to the specific fashion partner.

Eventually, *Digital Moda*'s US merchandisers were able to stimulate agreement from partner company merchandisers to showcase not only current but also past season fashion product in social commerce campaigns. Negotiations had also started at Milan headquarters to get exclusive consent from the existing roster of more than twenty fashion company partners (at the time) to incorporate Co-branding into future e-commerce agreements. The *culture premium* played a noteworthy role in extending the influence legitimacy of *Digital Moda*. *Pure Brand Unit* continued the tradition of developing perks for fashion companies to join social commerce, such as free editorial coverage on *DigitalModa.com*'s internal blog, or free banner ad placement on select fashion portals (e.g., Style.com, Elle.com) for the duration of a campaign.

At the end of each Co-branding campaign, *Digital Moda*'s US marketing team sought from the fashion partner in question to extend the terms of the agreement for experimenting with social commerce for another year. It was important for the *Partner Division* and the *Pure Brand Unit* to figure out how important was the culture premium as a practice in bringing influence legitimacy to the table. It was vital that *Digital Moda* and partner fashion companies 'play' with as many components of the Co-branding relationship, as possible. "We keep the evolving [Social Commerce] relationship, as this evolution is taking place, even though it does not generate much in sales", the Director of Marketing in the US offered, "because it does not cost us much. If it is a highly sought-after partnership with a fashion partner, we could also tell our [social commerce] publishers, that maybe we would have a minimum commitment where we would pay them, say, $5,000 per month to sponsor a display regularly for a coveted [fashion] brand".

Ultimately, at this stage of the legitimization game, keeping both sides, fashion companies and social commerce partners, happy in the Co-branding relationship was the simplest measure of influence legitimacy. "I know for a fact", the US Director of Marketing argued, "that the amount of visitors that [*StyleMag*] gets and the amount of sales we will get for our fashion partner is not as important as [*StyleMag*] being powered with our e-commerce functionality and our partner brand being powered with fashion editorials. If it is like that, then the terms could be in my favor". With this advantageous alignment between legitimizing narrative and practice, *Digital Moda* ensured that its two constituent partners in Co-branding were able to reach a relationship of interdependence that exhausted the likely potential of exit by any one of them and, at the same time, fostered a search for discovery of creative assets and adoption of new practice.

TRANSFERRING TECH CULTURE TO BRICK-AND-MORTAR MEDIA PUBLISHERS

During 2011–2012, *Digital Moda*'s US team recognized that there was an untapped opportunity in extending its pragmatic and influence legitimacy to established fashion publishers. The US team lobbied headquarters to commit an increasing share of revenue to developing Co-branding proposals directed at the online divisions of fashion magazines, such as *Marie Claire, Elle*, and *Vogue*. "We need to start working with Vogue", clarified the US Marketing Director in brainstorming session with his team, "but not only to do banner campaigns. Instead, do an integrated partnership in which every 3 months, for example, Vogue will choose one look and *DigitalModa.com*'s merchandisers will put out merchandise for this look".

At the time there was one precedent when *Samplemod* had struck a deal with Vogue USA to host curated items from Vogue's January 2010 issue. *Samplemod* had covered the greater share of campaign costs in agreement with the culture premium practice of e-commerce companies in fashion in their bid to extending pragmatic legitimacy in the field. Vogue US was the passive decision-maker; it had limited financial engagement, but substantial clout in the partnership. Vogue editors chose fashion products for the campaign, while *Samplemod* was responsible for investing in creative digital assets, such as linking fashion product and banners, and promoting the collaboration. Lastly, *Samplemod* covered the costs of hiring a 'pro digital studio' agency to tag selected fashion product and make it shoppable.

Digital Moda's approach was different. The US executive team pressed headquarters in Italy to approve a new plan through which *Digital Moda* would compel the online divisions of brick-and-mortar publishers to yield product-related and curatorial influence as part of a Co-branding relationship. The US team grew frustrated with the fact that banner advertising continued to be a major stronghold in the advertising budgets of established publishers on the Internet, even when their advertising divisions had made the transition to online publishing. Banner advertising had also briefly taken over the advertising budgets of fashion companies online, to make up for dwindling industry-wide print advertising budgets after 2008. "Even though our company now harbors access and manages online marketing for some of the most coveted brands in the world", the Director of Marketing in the US quipped in meetings with his 4-person team, "traditional editorials do not want to accept the behavior of their Social Commerce counterparts online. Publishing firms think; what is the cost of that and how much can be charge for it? The media industry has started to realize that it is productive to link product and content. But, they will never change, however they progress, *unless Digital Moda tells them how it works*".

In spite of *Digital Moda*'s established legitimacy in the fashion field by 2011, fashion companies had kept up the routine of spending money on banners. This was a tradition that grew out of placing adverts in the paper editions of fashion magazines. The costs of placing banner adverts online with their traditional publishers were lower than what fashion companies had paid for securing dedicated advertising space in paper editions. This fact made the established institutional routines stick. A luxury fashion company, comparable to Giorgio Armani, for instance, spent more than $3 million a year for buying dedicated advertising space in every paper issue of Vogue. In comparison, a basic banner with Style.com cost its Communication division 10 times less in 2011. *Digital Moda*'s US Marketing Director, a critical change agent in guiding the company's influencing initiatives with traditional magazines, was frustrated when headquarters in Italy commonly approached the US team with requests from fashion company partners for placing banner advertising. To executives in Digital Moda's *Pure Brand Unit* banner advertising represented a departed era that fashion companies still clung to, in keeping traditional sources of value and legitimacy afloat. The Director of Marketing in the US laid out the narrative to headquarters against fulfilling the needs of fashion partners for banner advertising. "We have decided"—he emphasized—"Display ads are obtrusive",

> It's uncalled for... even if technology has changed; at the end of the day it is still the most offensive way of advertising. You go to NYT.com and suddenly you get this stupid car in your face. I don't want to see that! It is better to spend money on awareness, but not purely of the banner ad form. We could do some banner ads in the future, but in a different way... like buying a page in a magazine and linking it online. Something that is more integrated. Let's do something that is more *meaningful* than just a stupid ad.

The Marketing Director's expectation was that fashion companies would not categorically shift their behavior in favor of Co-branding and curation campaigns, unless their established gatekeepers, fashion media publications did so, as well. "Magazines, like Vogue", he noted, "Are accustomed to dictate the rules of the game by selling exceptionally expensive ad space and treat it like Manhattan real estate. So, when [*Digital Moda*] approaches Elle and asks to do a 10 per cent revenue share campaign, Elle does not know what this means and asks: 'who is *Digital Moda*? How dare you tell me this?'"

On the other line, the Special Projects Coordinator at *Pure Brand* agreed. "So, when you are trying to offer something that is an integrated solution with the end consumer in mind", he added,

> Each department in Vogue needs to internally justify how the offer is good for them. The Editorial Director needs to figure out how the offer is going to be justified editorially. Business Development needs to know; OK, is this new partner that we are adding? Sales need to know – well, they are going to have 10,000 impressions on my site, but are they going to pay me the money I expect to be paid for banner ads? So, to be honest, these discussions can go on for 6 months easily.

The Special Projects Coordinator expected that future collaboration with traditional fashion media would have to be designed as a special case of

Co-branding, in which certain 'culture premium' rewards would have to be developed to incite immediate notice from publishers. After some iteration with headquarters, the US team reached a surprising decision in 2012, choosing against invoking the cultural premium practice. The US office had concluded that the terms of collaboration on any future agreements with traditional fashion media would, simply, have to respect the revenue-share culture that *Digital Moda* already used with social commerce publisher partners. Having accomplished the long road to legitimacy with established luxury fashion companies, *Digital Moda* was not going backwards. "We can give you this much money", offered in brainstorming meetings the US Marketing Director,

> The revenue depends on you and your content. You *need to work for your revenue. We need to wake them up to the fact* that $1 million imposes a ceiling. If banners are thought out as purely a short-term thing, then having this practice is okay. But, there is no sustainability in this approach. This is partly why we need more sustainable practices. When there is a curated shopping section, people understand that there is product proposal built around content, which is also sponsored by the magazine. We will never leave our idea of Co-branding and editorial integration. We would rather combine it with display.

Subsequent negotiations provided a fair amount of what fashion publishers probably found to be quite unexpected information. As per custom, *Digital Moda*'s marketing team in the US communicated the company's desire for publishers to loosen their siloed editorial, sales, and business development divisions. In formal meetings, the Special Projects Coordinator advised executives in business development for fashion publishers that their priorities online should be flipped and that their ability to source luxury fashion *product* from high-fashion brands with e-commerce properties was more important than their previous function of creating *content*. The vantage point of the industry had shifted to collaboration between e-commerce and social commerce and traditional fashion magazines were, apparently, late in the game. The Director of Marketing in the US office frequently pointed out internally that the gist of conversations with traditional fashion media should be to communicate to them that "the magazines should be happy that *they are given the opportunity* to work with [fashion] brands. The fashion partners in our portfolio will increase from 20 to 40 in only three years. And, if we see that this type of project works for us and *our* brands, we'd be the first to propose you to collaborate with us, but on our terms".

Digital Moda had, in essence, developed a united front against traditional fashion media and the main communiqué seemed to be that established fashion companies had been socialized to expecting social commerce partnerships. The marketing team at *Digital Moda*'s office in NYC rationalized that, if traditional fashion publishers stuck to their banner advertising approach, they would lose purchase in the field of digital fashion, similar to the situation experienced by Time Inc.'s StyleFind.com, due to their lack of contextual knowledge and pragmatic legitimacy in the new field. The final plug when talking to traditional fashion media was to point out *Digital Moda*'s long-standing moral and pragmatic legitimacy with fashion partners. The Director of Marketing was rather strong-minded:

> Publishers such as, say, Marie Claire, can either choose someone like StyleFind.com to collaborate with on finding styles and eventually linking to a third-party retailer, or can directly work with an individual brand or a retailer. We have the widest, deepest selection on the net. By going to us, you do not need to go to the aggregators. We have to be the one-stop-shop for all of your needs.

The US office determined that if, due to poor commercial performance in a Co-branding campaign, publishers were unable or unwilling to fulfill their guarantee to pay a designated performance commission to *Digital Moda*, the marketing team would reevaluate the terms under which fashion brand partners participated in future online advertising campaigns with the said traditional fashion media publisher. The long run view of the Director of Marketing in the US was that *Pure Brand* should push fashion magazines "to work harder, so that our brands can jump on the wagon, and not off the wagon". The plan also encouraged *Pure Brand Unit* to caution traditional fashion publishers that the latter would likely have very limited access to the online advertising budgets of fashion partners. In fact, online collaboration with a fashion company partner of *Digital Moda* would only probably happen once, and only through a Co-branding campaign, after a new fashion company had launched e-commerce. The new e-commerce Website would then be introduced by showcasing selected product by the fashion brand in question and matching the curation to an editorial copy, created by the

fashion magazine's editorial team. The collaboration would be performance-based and the success of the campaign would be determined by
the total traffic of unique visitors to the partner e-commerce Website, as
opposed to the number of impressions of a banner.

In Co-branding negotiations with traditional fashion media in 2011,
their newly founded online divisions were reluctant to accept these terms
of 'digital' engagement, since doing so predictably exposed them to
accommodating requests of a non-esthetic nature; namely, that their banners generated commercial results. "The publisher has never had to earn
advertising dollars", the Global Director of Marketing at *Digital Moda*
noted. "The publisher has created so much content in their lifetime that
they can now say, OK, $10,000 or $50,000 for a full-page ad". The
Special Projects Coordinator in *Pure Brand* further presumed that the
origins of this behavior were explained by the existence of gatekeeping
advantages, traditionally enjoyed by fashion publishers:

> If I want to do a Co-branding partnership with all the magazines, it's not a
> problem at all! If a new partner comes to the editors of Vogue and says: 'I
> want to power your shopping section and all the products that your editors
> curate; I am going to send my merchandise to you; you can put it up, so
> people can shop them. And I am going to give you $1,000,000 in fees'.
> You are not going to tell me no! The problem is *not whether the concept
> is being accepted or not*; the problem is that the whole concept is that we
> want to work with a partner who is not – we feel – taking our advertising
> money and saying, now I've got nothing else to do with you. This is the
> traditional behavior that they have, and we have to change it.

In sum, traditional fashion media were unaccustomed to viewing their
role as anything, but esthetic mediation. Established publishers (such as
Conde Nast's Vogue) typically agreed to terms of service with an advertiser (such as *Digital Moda*) on the basis of 'cost per impression' (CPI),
or 'cost per thousand impressions' (CPM) measure. This metric referred
to the price of 1000 advertising impressions on one webpage that an
advertiser paid per 1000 views of a banner ad by a unique visitor, regard-
less of whether the ad was clicked on, or not. Each appearance of the
image in front of a user counted as one 'impression'. In a CPM deal,
the hosting Website, typically publisher such as Vogue.com, displayed the
banner against payment for a total amount of impressions. e-commerce
and social commerce companies, however, preferred to collaborate on

'cost-per-click' (CPC) basis. CPC is an Internet advertising model, in which an advertiser pays a publisher when an ad is clicked. A 'click' transfers the viewer to the advertiser's Website. This type of contract is known as pay-for-performance advertising, whereby payment is triggered by a mutually agreed upon activity, such as a 'click', Website registration, or even, a sale.

CPM was a one-way street for displaying esthetic gatekeeper advantages by traditional fashion media, in which the publisher took no responsibility for sales performance. In contrast, in a CPC agreement, the payment was triggered by a mutually agreed upon action that presumed that added value was being sought by partners. *Digital Moda* had to persuade traditional fashion publishers to change their most fundamental behavior of doing business. It seemed that to influence fashion magazine publishers, *Digital Moda* had decided on a different legitimizing approach; one, in which the company asserted its own importance in the fashion field, instead of making financial adjustments for the benefit of bridging the gap in culture with counterparts. "I of course know, what the issue is about", the Director of Marketing offered on many occasions when discussing *Digital Moda*'s rapport with traditional fashion media publishers:

> There is a disconnect between how an E-Commerce retailer thinks and how publishers think. When this person [publisher] hears of 10 per cent commission, all they can think about is CPM. And, I'm like, dude, if you push it, you can earn money through commissions. And, that person thinks, if I push it, and there are 100,000 impressions, I will earn $200. The issue is, that even though they do think of all these factors, you just look at a retailer with a '$' sign. Unfortunately, they don't think about the editorial and marketing spillovers to their own brand and business.

The spoiler alert for the next section is that *Digital Moda's Pure Brand Unit* returned to a softer approach to influencing publishers, somewhat akin to employing the culture premium inducement—bridging gaps in culture through financial incentives. The compromise was that to compensate for the institutionalized behavior of traditional fashion publishers, *Digital Moda* would agree to pay a two-, three-, or six- month 'flat fee' to ascertain that publishers transformed their cultural prerogatives in the direction of Co-branding. "I think the best is to get a big player", explained the Special Projects Coordinator. "I don't mind paying $50K to Elle, even though this is not going to be the perfect thing for me. But, if we strike this deal, then all the smaller guys, who are playing 'little rascals', will be persuaded to work with us and we can then leverage". The next sections describe how this precise transition was accomplished.

PURE BRAND UNIT AND VOGUE ITALY

Vogue Italy is occasionally referred to as "the world's most influential fashion magazine" and is, in addition, considered to be the least commercial of Condé Nast's publications (Angeletti et al. 2012). Between 2010 and 2012, *Digital Moda* and Vogue Italy conceived of a long-term partnership in Co-branding—the first of its kind between an e-commerce fashion company and a traditional fashion publisher. *Digital Moda*'s marketing team in the US designed the campaign. Seeking influence legitimacy, the Special Projects Coordinator at the *Pure Brand Unit* activated negotiations with Vogue's business development and editorial teams. Vogue Italy accepted a flat fee for promoting visual banners associated with the Co-branding campaign. Additionally, Vogue Italy signed a revenue share agreement with *Digital Moda*. Through this modified culture premium, an important curatorial milestone was achieved. Online merchandisers in *Digital Moda* gained the ability to exert veto power over Vogue Italy editors. Online editors at Vogue had to check in with merchandisers in *Digital Moda* each time that Vogue's team decided to change any of the featured fashion items in the collaboration, picked from *Digital Moda*'s fashion partners' e-commerce sites during the period. The *Partner Division* team, furthermore, reached out to existing fashion partners and asked their e-commerce teams and merchandisers about the fashion product that would be 'appropriate' to feature on the co-branded e-commerce section between *Digital Moda* and Vogue Italy.

The ability that *Digital Moda* gained in manipulating curation decisions demonstrated that the company had growing influence legitimacy, stemming from its expanding relationship with fashion brands. The Special Projects Coordinator in *Pure Brand* explained this division of labor between the parties during the campaign:

> The products that we curate with you can be taken out of *DigitalModa. com*; *Digiluxe.com*; or, any of the clients we have. Vogue does not have the product, and the consumer goes directly to shop on our front. It is something that fashion editors from Social Commerce partners already

do directly on our site: picking independently products to feature editorially on their web fronts. So, obviously, if [*CommunityMag*] or [*StyleMag*] decided to do the same partnership as Vogue, since we already have partnerships with them through LinkShare, their editors would freely select this product directly from the product listing. Our advantage with Vogue is that we do it *for* them.

Logistically, the partnership continued between 2010 and 2012 and *Digital Moda*'s Italian team created a mini shoplet hosted on www. Vogue.it, Vogue's main online property in the EU. In 2012, *Digital Moda* broadened the partnership by augmenting the editorial role of its own merchandisers and online editors at *the Pure Brand Unit*, who took the lead on creating online editorials for a rotating "look of the week" at Vogue Italy. Thus, Digital Moda's legitimacy had expanded from a pragmatic legitimacy associated with linking to product, through to an influence legitimacy of editorializing with Vogue. "The idea is that there is an editorial component in the collaboration", said of the augmented relationship the Global Marketing Director at *Digital Moda*. "We totally have their input re: what trends to feature". The US CEO of *Digital Moda*, who was among the proponents of Co-branding with publishers, like Vogue, explained that this first collaboration was all about esthetics, and "honestly, awareness. You go to Vogue to look at pictures, not to shop. But, the awareness part should not be underestimated, because awareness creates future sales. It's a mutual thing. *They provide the content; we have the product*".

The partnership held a major momentum for influence legitimacy. "No one has done it with Vogue Italy", the CEO in the US noted. To underscore the difference in influence legitimacy gained by *Digital Moda* over time across the two contexts—US and Europe—the CEO added, "We tried with the American Vogue, but the publishing industry in Italy is much more developed than the US. They can see the value of novelty. The Americans are just after the money". In other words, as the least commercial of Condé Nast's publications, Vogue Italy presented a trickier case for yielding editorial control. Comfortable with the relationship, in 2012 the partners focused on particular brands that editors and merchandisers wanted to promote. One example was the "Pink Tartan" Co-branding campaign, featuring fashion product from *Digiluxe.com* and creative editorials designed by *Digital Moda* USA. The editorials included photo-shoots and fashion content designed by merchandisers at the US office with engagement from editors in Vogue Italy. The campaign was topped off with an advertising banner, a click away from the Co-branded collection.

By March 2012, Vogue Italy had become the partner of choice for *Digital Moda*, when announcing the launch of new fashion partner e-commerce Websites or, in this case, the launch of another new e-commerce property by *Digital Moda*. The group had launched a footwear e-commerce fashion property in 2012 and its inauguration was broadcasted by a special collaboration between Vogue Italy and *Digital Moda* via Facebook. This was yet another new development in fashion publishing. The campaign was developed by merchandisers and editors in *Digital Moda*'s US office. The Facebook page of the new e-commerce property footwear highlighted daily product galleries in a series introducing the theme behind the curated selection of product. The product gallery was curated by a "stylist of the week" picked by *Digital Moda*'s merchandisers, in close collaboration with Vogue Italy. A click on the Facebook gallery in which an online personal assistant called "Ms. Suzie" also offered advice, led users to a dedicated e-commerce space on Vogue Italy, where the product could be reviewed and purchased. This type of collaboration in editorial and product curation opened Vogue Italy up to a new conceptualization of using digital assets in their practice.

Pure Brand Unit and Women's Wear Daily (WWD)

During the first quarter of 2011, executives in the US office reported that a positive development on an advertising deal had taken place between *Digital Moda* and Women's Wear Daily (WWD), one of the top-25 globally visited fashion and entertainment Websites. The campaign was scheduled to coincide with Spring/Summer 2012 Fashion Week in Milan, and the commercial aspect of the partnership was to trigger traffic from WWD's home page to shopping pages of fashion brand partners housed on *Digiluxe.com*, *Digital Moda*'s youngest e-commerce property. The result from this partnership was, as the industry called it, a creative "overtake" of WWD home page in September 2011. The partnership was titled "overtake" because Digital Moda's web team handcrafted a digital solution in which the background of WWD's Website, WWD.com was reshaped with the creative color background of *Digiluxe. com*, complete with links to fashion product and brands from *Digiluxe. com*. The background displayed a series of dynamic images that incited the viewer to visit *Digiluxe.com*, view a fashion video by a celebrated photographer, and 'mouse-hover' over links that, if clicked, led to the current season collections of select designers on *Digiluxe.com*.

The solution developed by *Digital Moda*'s technology team in the US was ingenious in an esthetic sense. By "overtaking" the partner's own Website background, the team circumvented traditional banner display and instead, employed the concept of floating image-laden background and text links in a dazzling manifestation of Co-branding logic, in which the two brands merged. In exchange for exposing WWD to this novel esthetic experience, and in compliance with the cultural premium approach with publishers, *Digital Moda* decided to honor WWD's request to base the partnership on a cost per impression (CPM) basis. *Digital Moda*'s European headquarters were not too ecstatic to give the deal a go-ahead, because this entrepreneurial opportunity would register as a financial loss to the company, owing to the CPM deal. In addition to financing and creating the technical solution for the Co-branding page, *Digital Moda*'s US team had to augment the culture premium incentive by paying a CPM fee to WWD, the collaborating party. Predictably, US executives argued that they remained willing to finance the deal, in exchange for gaining influence legitimacy, and showcasing the motivation of this traditional content publisher to accept new culture. Here was the hook: in return for this high-risk Co-branding initiative, *Digital Moda*'s marketing team requested from WWD executives full creative control over the "overtake" solution. This included the deployment of creative web development assets, the curation of fashion brands from *Digiluxe. com* for the background "overtake", and the selection of product that was a click away from the user once they hovered over a brand name in the background. The marketing team in the US office reasoned cautiously that the impact of the overtake would be positive, creating legitimacy results for *Digital Moda* and its youngest brand property, *Digiluxe.com*:

> Well, the new site format of WWD is much better. If nothing, it will give us visibility... Before, it had a click-thru[2] of 1.5 percent; now, the banner click-thru has jumped to 2.8 per cent. It is good that the campaign also coincides with Fashion Week in Italy. The campaign is both about traffic, and more cultural awareness about the brands on *Digiluxe.com*.

One particular episode just days before the "overtake" reveals how far *Digital Moda* was prepared to venture in order to exploit this initiative to successfully introduce new culture into the toolset of practice at WWD. On a Friday in September 2011, only two days before the "overtake", the US Marketing Director was informed that WWD's web team had contracted an outside vendor to handle the placement of dynamic text links for the campaign. The text links were easy to code for WWD, or certainly, for *Digital Moda*. However, the fact that, contrary to agreement, this task was outsourced to an outside vendor, effectively undermined *Digital Moda*'s co-'ownership' in the collaboration. The background text links that WWD's web team had to code, featured temporary access to proprietary API codes for *Digiluxe.com*, which would now be granted to outsiders.

Upon learning this, the Marketing Director in the US requested help from the Global Marketing Division at headquarters. "They requested an outside vendor", she explained to colleagues, "because they say their site is very 'Rich Media' and they need special help with that for the dynamic placement of brand links". The US Marketing Director in 2012 had held the position only for a few months and had noticed that *Digital Moda* typically "owned" the creative process in Co-branding collaborations related to web development. The request by WWD was unusual. She needed an interpretation from headquarters. Two reasons stand out if we try to explain why *Digital Moda*'s US executives preferred to be responsible for even ostensibly insignificant technical features of projects whose goal was to change the culture of publishers. The first reason was to signal to traditional fashion publishers that *Digital Moda* was, indeed, "a one-stop-shop for everything digital".[3] The other motivation was that US executives had assigned importance on growing the influence of the company with traditional fashion media publishers. WWD was a well-known publisher and mediator of fashion content and product, and this strategic branding project had to be executed at the highest level of technical specification. The potential effect of this partnership on the influence legitimacy of *Digital Moda* could not be overstated.

The online marketing team at *Digital Moda* US was the unit that handled governance problems in online collaborations. During a highly technical, yet leverage-provoking call, the US Director of Marketing clarified to WWD's web development team in the US that acting on behalf of *Digital Moda* on any technical tasks during the development period should have been cleared with the US team. "Will you serve the images as a tag or a static image, if you were to produce them?" started the web expert at WWD. "We will serve the images as a URL", a member from

Digital Moda's marketing team responded. The web expert then asked: "the links to fashion brands have to be served by a Rich Media vendor. Do you do this usually?" The *Digital Moda* marketing expert was surprised at this request, "No, we usually do not work with any outside vendors when we serve *our own site* [i.e., *Digiluxe.com*]". WWD's team then clarified that "because our website is so rich in flash media, an outside rich media vendor *can know how to create* the type very quickly".

The implication from this conversation was that *Digital Moda*'s team was not expected to have expertise in handling Rich Media content. WWD's development team had revealed this by asking: "*Do you do this usually?*" This was a complex question for *Digital Moda*'s marketing team to answer. On the one hand, if WWD's web development team had requested at the start of collaboration that *Digital Moda* produce Rich Media links, the US team would have been upset, for being perceived as a pure technology company. At headquarters, the Global Marketing Director was clear on the official position on this leverage point: "We never promote *Digital Moda* as a service provider. We are not GSI Commerce.[4] In other words, we use WWD for promoting campaigns for our luxury fashion partners that *Digiluxe.com* hosts". The reluctance of *Digital Moda*'s executive team to associate their influence legitimacy with that of an e-commerce consultant—which was part of the larger skillset—verbalizes the company's substantive evolution from a discounted retailer and e-commerce service provider to an e-commerce fashion conglomerate with a founding competence in many areas of this practice.

The marketing team at the US office decided to explain its influence legitimacy directly to the outside vendor, contracted by WWD. The Director of Marketing phoned the agency selected by WWD, and explained to its executive team that, "this is the first time we are working with someone else. *We usually manage our own campaigns*". A member of *Digital Moda*'s web development team spent time during the weekend to ensure that the agency executed to specification and served Rich Media content. During the weekend, the web developer learned from the agency that this was not the first time that their services had been requested by WWD. In fact, the agency's conclusion provided valuable insight to the marketing team at *Digital Moda* in that, per agency's web development team "WWD is not in the business of overdrawing their own tech resources for someone else's *banner* hosting". By outsourcing the work, and thus revealing to others *Digital Moda*'s proprietary API codes, WWD deliberately maintained a degree of cultural reserve with regard to the collaboration.

This was a critical piece of contextual information for *Digital Moda*'s marketing team. Avoiding understanding or honoring technology commitments to actual partners, such as *Digital Moda*, demonstrated the desire for control by WWD over the implementation of Co-branding projects. This perspective was very similar to how *MilanModa1* had managed its own e-commerce experiment. Vogue Italy and WWD, in sum, provided two very different experiences and proved to be two very different partners, but the challenge in the days ahead, despite measurable success produced by the "overtake" campaign, in this latter case, continued to be to harvest change in the culture of traditional fashion publishers.

PURE BRAND UNIT AND A GLOBAL FASHION MEDIA PUBLISHER

A final example of securing influence legitimacy with traditional media publishers is the negotiation between *Digital Moda* and one of the largest global media publishing companies on a long-term Co-branding collaboration, in 2011. The media conglomerate owned magazines, newspapers and had assets in numerous domains, which included four of USA's largest monthly fashion publications. The CEO and the marketing team in the US office met with high-ranking executives from the digital arm of the publishing corporation. The publisher's team included a Project Management leader, editors in two of the publisher's principal fashion magazines, and the Chief Revenue Officer. *Digital Moda*'s US team was partial to possible partnership with this publisher because the latter was actively experimenting within the digital field of fashion, and had, in addition, acquired one of the top-10 social commerce companies in fashion. Initial discussions between the two parties, held at the offices of *Digital Moda* in NYC, revealed that the media executives were open to exploiting *Digital Moda*'s influence in Co-branding.

One unusual aspect in the negotiations was the explicitness of the publisher to align its vision of Co-branding with that of *Digital Moda*. As in other collaborations, the marketing team at *Digital Moda* expected to have relative autonomy in a future partnership that would extend to autonomy in selecting editorial themes and pairing them with fashion product. Executives at the US office were impressed with the quality of the collaboration proposal from the publishing company. The US

Marketing Director concluded that the conglomerate was looking to "impress" *Digital Moda*'s marketing team by coming up with a diverse set of action items for a partnership. The conglomerate had already endeavored to partner with two other highly visible social commerce startups in 2011. The solution developed by these startups linked visitors to the online fashion magazine properties, owned by the conglomerate, with fashion product from affiliated e-commerce retailers. The problem appeared to be that the publishing conglomerate did not have consistent access to luxury fashion product, derived from the e-commerce Websites of luxury fashion brands.

A mix of ideas was offered by the publisher, whose executives had come prepared with glossy brochures, in the two meetings that occurred in *Digital Moda*'s offices. Among these were collaborations between *Digital Moda* and fashion magazines on curating "daily deals", developing a "look of the week" that featured selected fashion product, and, "shopping the video". The preliminary proposal by the publisher detailed that *Digital Moda* would curate fashion product from its e-commerce properties and the e-commerce Websites of its fashion partners, and tailor the product to seasonal Fashion Guides put forth during the year by the four fashion magazines, owned by the conglomerate. A second part of the proposal, as was typical for Co-branding partnerships, was to let *Digital Moda* develop an e-commerce solution that allowed visitors to browse editorial content and "click to purchase" curated fashion items available on *Digital Moda*'s brand partner Websites. The media conglomerate team appeared to have advanced understanding of Co-branding, and, thus, the partnership appealed to *Digital Moda*'s development team. The "custom video trunk show", for example, was a new method for delivering marketing messages and was in line with *Digital Moda*'s advocacy for increased use of shoppable video content in partnerships. "We agree to this; it's part of our strategy", said the US Marketing Director. An executive from *Pure Brand*, likewise, reported that the publisher's team was, moreover, "currently the only people that *Digital Moda has felt they share the same language* with". These similarities in thinking made it difficult to reject the proposal.

However, the intention of the long-term partnership was not to pursue an exclusive relationship. *Digital Moda* would be one of several e-commerce fashion retailers that would place fashion product links on the publisher's online glossies. As expected, this situation was untenable for the US team. The US CEO requested that *Digital Moda* be the sole Co-branding partner. US executives predictably focused the remaining conversation on their exclusive access to a growing number of luxury fashion brands, their gatekeeping role in curating vast collections of branded fashion product, and, the all-encompassing skillset of *Digital Moda* in developing an exclusive collection of digital marketing assets. The Director of Marketing in the US summarized for the publisher's representative team the only acceptable terms of an agreement for *Digital Moda*:

> [The two magazines] get approximately 2.5 million per month visitor traffic. And, this traffic comes from fashion-sensitive shoppers. So, this is a brand-building initiative for us. I realize that most of this will be browsing, but when you read about fashion on any of these magazines and you can buy it immediately, it's a bonus. *Digital Moda* wants all that is proposed by [the partner] to be *shoppable*. And, we want all curated fashion product to be by our fashion partners.

The deal-breaker in the proposal was the request by the media conglomerate that *Digital Moda* pay $1 million for six months' worth of impressions based on a CPM deal if it were to be the only partner in the Co-branding collaboration. *Digital Moda*'s Marketing Director began suspecting that behind the sophisticated façade of the proposal, the publisher still assumed that theirs was an authoritative status and that any perceived "outsiders" to their gatekeeper status, had to pay for the privilege of accessing fashion magazine content. "Their proposal still looked like an advertising pitch, rather than a genuine understanding or E-Commerce", the Director of Marketing concluded. "Structurally, they still act as a publisher. Which is what's wrong with it".

After a two-month deliberation, *Digital Moda* rejected the proposal on the count that, as one executive at headquarters said, it was "piecemeal and did not have the full array of integrated ideas that we would be comfortable with responding to". The US executive team reached an interesting conclusion. The publishing conglomerate, the US CEO asserted, had designed the proposal in mind with gaining legitimacy for its own business online by "hoarding traffic from *Digital Moda* as a recognized fashion player online". An example was the envisaged exposure to Facebook. The proposal intended the design of a social media campaign for one of the largest fashion glossies in the conglomerate's portfolio, which had then amassed 32,000 fans on Facebook. The proposal specified that *Digital Moda* would partner for a summer campaign with the magazine through Facebook. The problem was that future shoppers would gain access to a curated selection of fashion product from the e-commerce properties of fashion brand partners of *Digital Moda*, only if they became "fans" of the magazine on Facebook. The proposed terms seemed to be more value enhancing for the other partner. As per the US Marketing Director, publishers in the fashion industry had reached the limits of their own legitimacy; yet, still held on to the desire for excessive control in a superior–subordinate relationship with advertisers. The game had changed and *Digital Moda*'s influence legitimacy with fashion companies could be used as leverage:

> Having the brands gives us a lot of power when we deal with the magazines. When editors give us something in terms of content, we give them something in terms of product. Obviously, after 6 years of partnerships, we are able to tell them, OK let's do these types of campaigns. We have 6-year partnership with Vogue. We are now in a position to tell our brands: look, we now have long-term partnerships with these publishers, and work like an agency. So, if you're interested in having a digital partnership with them, you can pass through us instead of going directly to them. This is a good position for us. We can say to them [publishers] in return; when you make the partnership with us, you actually make it with the rest of our 21 [at the time] brands. These brands will always be interested in making campaigns with you.

In the two months during which *Digital Moda*'s US team discussed engagement with the publisher, the executive team expressed concern that in the long run, large consolidated publishing media firms would end up using cookie-cutter approach when managing the online advertising relationships for the fashion magazines that they owned. Magazines held by one publishing group typically functioned as independent profit centers and their corporate owner preferred to cap on established revenue sources from banner advertising, rather than opting for experimenting. Under the umbrella of publishers, fashion glossies gone online would become indistinguishable from one another. *Digital Moda*'s team in the US was wary of engaging with a publisher that did "not want to experiment too much". Correspondingly, *Digital Moda*'s Chief Branding Consultant, a long-term fashion editor and industry insider who occasionally visited the US office to provide strategic advice, summed up her concerns regarding future partnerships with media publishers. "We don't want to niche-fy [cluster] all of our brands into one property. This is my biggest concern".

After rejecting the publisher's proposal in late 2011, *Digital Moda*'s marketing team decided that in future negotiations, they would put forward two points to publishers. Said the Marketing Director, "Number one is that there is a need for e-commerce with each of these players; and, number two is that *we* are the E-Commerce provider". Based on this new policy narrative, established publishers had to agree on these two points before negotiations. The Director of Marketing considered that this statement, firm as it was, would epitomize the influence legitimacy of *Digital Moda* in the fashion field. If the two points were ever to be agreed upon by established publishers, he projected that "*this probably will send a huge signal throughout the [online] community*". "They will figure out how to take these businesses to the next level", the Director of Marketing finally submitted. "The big media firms will get consolidated with the smaller high-tech. But, this does not mean that the former will become super innovative, because innovation trickles down, and we are *the* innovator".

Notes

1. CEO, *Digital Moda*, USA.
2. In Web advertising, click-through represents the action by a visitor who clicks on an advertisement and goes to the advertiser's Website. The click-through rate measures the amount of times an ad is clicked versus the amount of times it's been viewed but not clicked (impression). Source: www.webopedia.com.
3. Recall, that both the US Director of Marketing and the Director of the *Partner Division* had a perfectly aligned perspective of this, main legitimating narrative by Digital Moda.
4. GSI Commerce Inc. is one of the world's largest e-commerce contractors owned by eBay since 2011.

Bibliography

Angeletti, N., Oliva, A., & Wintour, A. (2012). *In vogue: An illustrated history of the world's most famous fashion magazine.* New York: Rizzoli.

Google Commerce Blog. (2011). *Enhancing shopping experience on Google.* Retrieved from: https://commerce.googleblog.com/2011/09/enhancing-shopping-experience-on-google.html [16 July 2017].

Powell, W.W. (2012). Expanding the scope of institutional analysis. In DiMaggio, P.J., & Powell, W.W. (Eds.), *The new institutionalism in organizational analysis*, 183–201. Chicago, IL: University of Chicago Press.

Suchman, M. (1995). Managing legitimacy, strategic & institutional approaches. *Academy of Management Review, 20*(3), 571–610.

Suddaby, R., & Greenwood, R. (2005). Rhetorical strategies of legitimacy. *Administrative Science Quarterly, 50*(1), 35–67.

CHAPTER 7

Ethnography at the Threshold:
A Confessional on Theory and Method

Entering the emerging field of high-tech e-commerce fashion was very different from grabbing for purchase into the magisterial domain of high fashion. Both entries provided me with a challenging, and ultimately, fascinating familiarity about the workings of each. I entered the fashion field at a very chaotic point in its responses to e-commerce adaptation. In e-commerce, the new field of digital fashion had exploded. The competence of new players under scrutiny in the book was becoming more easily documented, but the complexity of their thinking and subsequent action was unfolding in elaborate social situations, which could only be studied by observation. As we established, collaboration between e-commerce and social commerce peers alone was a complicated social situation, in which partners gave up and gained contextual knowledge and formed new practices on the basis of this contextual learning-by-doing. Similarly, depending on their role in the organizational structure, executives in fashion companies swerved in-between thinking about whether to hinder or accept e-commerce, providing overwhelmingly elaborate and, at times, fairly emotional responses.

I started out by following the formal judgments of opinion-makers in luxury fashion, interviewing a fair amount of independent industry experts, digital agencies, luxury consultancies, and flagship luxury associations (e.g., *Fondazione Altagamma*, Walpole, USDA). To further understand the prerogatives of players in the ecology around luxury fashion, I participated in many and varied fashion industry events, such as the *Luxury Interactive* conference, held each year in London and

New York, *Fashion 2.0* organized by the Style Coalition in NYC, and, of course, in pairing business with the pleasures of graduate school, I participated in the annual meetings of the *Luxury Club* at Columbia Business School, NYU Stern School of Business, and Harvard Business School. Paying attention to beliefs advanced by these organizations permitted to track the evolution in the behavior of their fashion clients with regard to e-commerce.

I also entered the field knowing that early sociologists had hypothesized that fashion was a phenomenon of fundamental sociological importance for "human group life" (Blumer 1969, p. 275) and that the field, evidently, influenced the "central content of any field in which it operates" (ibid., p. 277). The field of fashion held court over the display of socio-economic status and the production of culture of wearability that heralded each incoming economic age in modern society. Simmel (1957) had proposed that a "trickle down" mechanism of diffusion of fashions existed, according to which fashions flowed vertically from the upper to the lower classes, with each social class being influenced by a higher social class in a remarkable process of product adoption, called social "imitation". The study of fashion in the twentieth century was further extended by Blumer, who reframed the formation of fashion tastes and styles as a process of "collective selection" of a few fashions from various competing alternatives. Groups of people simply responded to the "direction of modernity" (1969, p. 280), instead of clutching to the notion of furthering one's class distinction. I also had a soft spot for Hebdige (1979), who finally and famously, introduced the idea that fashion was a form of refutation of existing class and power relations in society, brought on by spectacular youth subcultures that articulated illicit content in prohibited forms.

Later, Davis (1992) moved from this more fundamental thinking about fashion to attempting to describe its underlying industry. He found that the fashion industry was a system with a distinct innovative central core, represented by a select group of designers, and from this center innovations and modifications radiated outward to fashion consumers. Yet, this innovative central core responsible for design was fragile and its ability to "innovate" was circumscribed by the intersecting volatility of changing industry, economic conditions, and consumer behavior and tastes. I learned this during my very first attending of the National Retail Federation's (NRF) 2010 annual meeting. Within fashion companies, an interesting shift had ostensibly occurred, in which fashion merchandisers, and not designer-créateurs, had gained momentum in decision-making. This knowledge prompted asking where was, then, the "pure" expression of creative intent that actually accounted for the singular identity of fashion companies? What happened, if their executives were prompted, for example, by institutional changes in technology?

There was, in short, something truly uncontrollable, forcefully rebellious, but altogether, orderly traditional about this field. I learned that the conceptual reality of fashion organizations is one in which the fashion industry swung "between the artistic field and the economic field" (Bourdieu and Delsaut 1975, p. 22). The presence of both artistic and commercial rhetoric apparently left fashion companies in a discomforting management impasse "between cosmotheism and the doctrine of inherent differentiation" (Simmel 1957, p. 542). On the one hand, the production of clothing and accessory artifacts imbued with the ascribed features of craftsmanship, quality, and tradition was and still is viewed and promoted as an aesthetic economy (Entwistle and Rocamora 2006; Crane 2012) with no commercial considerations; a practice Bourdieu and Delsaut (1975, p. 28) have called "transubstantiation". On the other hand, the fashion industry is a highly globalized field of commerce that bridges "multiple networks that connect an upstream of suppliers to a downstream of customers through a market interface made of producers" (Aspers and Godart 2013, p. 181). Professional fashion organizations and industry practitioners—fashion companies, retail consultancies, flagship luxury organizations, designers, associations, advertising and publishing companies, and global communications divisions in fashion firms—took advantage of this implicit division between aesthetic and commercial labor. Creative Directors, Communications Directors, and Head Designers, embodied roles in the organizational structure that seemed to influence the aesthetic direction of fashion companies and give priority to the work of designer artists. Research had made little progress outside of these organizational domains of creativity. The silent hypothesis was that executives in other parts of the formal organizational structure in fashion companies, such as in merchandising, retail, and advertising, were tied up in a commercial enterprise (Aspers and Godart 2013).

On the other side of this spectrum, I discovered a completely new organizational field in the making—that of e-commerce and social commerce fashion companies. These players had all emergent identities and permitted an easier and far less formal entry. The fledgling Internet entrepreneurs used e-commerce technology to start their own fashion-slash-technology businesses, grappling with competing ideas of validating themselves as brand destinations and marketing channels. Some of them, like *Digital Moda*, had become key players in e-commerce fashion and were eager to share their struggles, hopes, and strategy with what they perceived to be a sympathetic ear. *Digital Moda*, in particular, had gained responsibility for formulating the e-commerce strategy for more than two-dozen (at the time I started my research) luxury fashion brands. This had, incredibly, happened without the company having had access to fashion organizations, publications, or retailers when it started. This field was evolving right in front of me, in New York's Silicon Alley, and this is where I ultimately hung my hat. These newcomers—with *Digital Moda* at the helm—were not direct competitors of fashion firms. However, their founders frequently referred to these entrepreneurial creations as "the new fashion brands" and "a *new generation*" of fashion businesses. These companies were able to discover a competitive advantage and a cultural identity based on the persuasive argument that their competency was dual, *both* in fashion and technology. The theoretically inspired curiosities were manifold. How were these "outsiders" able to sow sedition in the traditional fashion industry? How were they able to bridge the enormous gap that existed between them and the institutionalized realm of fashion companies?

I simply, "plunged", as Bruce Kogut—one of my advisors at Columbia Business School wittily suggested—into the vibrant waters of these start-ups in the digital field of fashion. My access to *Digital Moda* grew out of multiple contacts I developed through email, and during my attendance at industry conferences. I ultimately met with the (then) Director of Marketing and the CEO in the United States and set the stage for my extended ethnography. As I made progress in discovering *Digital Moda*'s place in this emerging ecology, the demography of the new field expanded before me. I knew that, theoretically, in such emerging ecologies, knowledge was produced contextually. By accumulating narrative data and knowledge on the capabilities and vision of e-commerce founders and executives in digital fashion, I could draw a sketch of their attempts to legitimate in the fashion industry.

Whatever their case for legitimation was, I hypothesized that these players had certain characteristics embedded in their formal organizational structure, roles, or practice that I originally designated to have a "*critical-enabling role*" in fashion. E-commerce and social commerce companies were the primary creators and users (von Hippel 1994) of new technology. This was an originating advantage that would allow them to develop dominant narratives around the use of new technology within their creative community. Eventually, the dominant narratives would spread out, to "nurture" and educate potential adopters of the value of new practice (Garud and Karnøe 2003; Shah and Tripsas 2007). In short, e-commerce and social commerce start-ups would co-construct the new field by relying on simple organizational structures and straightforward roles; build and share best practices in the field; and, facilitate the transition of fashion incumbents to adopting new digital practices in their cultural repertoire. As the reader no doubt appreciates, there still remained few key programmatic questions. How could *outsiders* to an institutionalized cultural terrain, like the fashion industry, influence the behavior of established fashion companies? Did their executives or founders collectively interpret the value of e-commerce for fashion companies and, later, thoughtfully share them with incumbents? So few of them had made the cut in becoming part of the ecology of organizations in digital fashion and the task seemed gargantuan. I started with a few solid conceptual proposals that proved to be guiding influence in my research design and implementation.

First, I examined the proposition by March et al. (1991) that, however "meager" the experience of these new organizations was, their strength (also an advantage for the researcher) was their ability to learn by accumulating a whole lot of knowledge from single, infrequent events in their life histories. Even trivial knowledge was likely to be interpreted richly and detailed stories would be woven around experiences. Indeed, I learned that this valuable idea of *learning-by-obsessively-documenting-and-doing* was at the heart of everyday work routines in this emerging demography of organizations in the new field of digital fashion—from *Luxemod* to *Samplemod*. Organizational ethnography and in-depth interviews proved to be suitable in this case precisely, when the new population was emergent and small in numbers. As my ethnography and interviews suggested, the small sample of very active e-commerce and social commerce players developed expertise and practice in their areas in a remarkably short time. The few actors were first-movers in the space. The need of their executives was to extensively document the successes and failures in their practice; to communicate with each other; and to, subsequently, agree on a dominant interpretation regarding the value of their respective businesses for established fashion companies. The knowledge that I, as an ethnographer, attempted to discover about the organizational practices in the field, extended in real time as executives wove their narratives, asked questions, and engaged in prolific discussions with one another. The ethnography and interviews allowed me to circumscribe the boundaries of the field as it evolved, and aggregate what I was learning about the field into a narrative that described its underlying social processes.

Second, my research took an in-depth ethnographic plunge into the cultural practices of a key engineer of e-commerce that had influenced both the behavior of peers in the community and of established fashion companies. Subsequently, the player in question—*Digital Moda*—became one of the largest e-commerce fashion retailers worldwide. At the time that I started probing in the field, *Digital Moda* had already signed exclusive e-commerce agreements with numerous international high-fashion brands. The underlying unremitting question continued to plague me: how did this company—a fashion outsider, at first—achieve such prominent standing with fashion brands and within its own community in digital fashion? My effort at conceptualizing *Digital Moda*'s role in the ecology benefitted from an important finding by Vedres and Stark (2010). They had discovered that when certain organizational actors became embedded at a "structural fold" in a social network—the network property of a cohesive group whose membership overlaps with that of another cohesive group—the role of these actors could take on multiple affiliations *at the same time*. Vedres and Stark had called such actors "multiple insiders, facilitating familiar access to diverse resources" (2010, p. 1150). This was an important point of conceptual inference, which proved to denote the temporal and cognitive proximity of *Digital Moda* as an institutional entrepreneur in the new field, explaining the ability of executives in this company to influence the direction of legitimation at other e-commerce and social commerce players, at the same time as *Digital Moda* influenced the adoption of new practice in fashion companies.

The primary location of my ethnography at *Digital Moda* was at its offices in NYC, and obviously I also traveled to headquarters in Milan. The main ethnography location in NYC was fitting, because headquarters tasked the US office to serve as incubator for experimenting with new e-commerce technologies and practice. The prime change agents in the company were stationed here and they excitedly supplied me with their evolving narratives on the role of e-commerce technology in fashion. During my extended ethnography at *Digital Moda*, I carried out in-depth interviews with key functions in both offices, spanning multiple strategic and operational domains, such as CEO, Global and US Directors of Marketing, Chief Technology Evangelist, buyers, merchandisers, editors, and co-founder crew. Careful longitudinal qualitative observations, along with interviews in the two contexts (and a healthy dose of internal documents, press releases, client presentations, commercial and customer plans, strategy plans, confidential agreements, media presentations and collaboration proposals by other parties), allowed me to assess how executives at *Digital Moda* viewed the company's functional and aesthetic value in the field (which, for the purposes of data analysis, I termed "internal identity"), and its "external identity"—the position executives held with regard to how they thought they were viewed by others (peers and fashion companies).

Third, I was dealing with two types of organizations; and, thus, two samples—established fashion companies and e-commerce and social commerce companies. I had to decipher where these populations intersected; figure out the cultural beliefs of executives in key digital start-ups; make sense of resulting practices and interpretations of peers in the emerging organizational field; and, study responses from fashion incumbents. On this last point, it seemed valuable to heed Burawoy's (1998, p. 5) direction to sample fashion companies for the study on the basis of a manageable "population of social situations" that certain players were in the thick of, rather than sample on the basis of age, size, craftsmanship, etc. My scrutinizing of a population of social situations during the longitudinal ethnography and interviews, instead of hunting for a preset sample, yielded five luxury fashion companies that represented different geographical fashion markets, with a common point of origin in the major cultural and commercial centers of high fashion—Milan, London, Paris, and New York. The five case studies proved to be examples of a typology of practice for some of the most visible international high-fashion brands producing both *haute couture* and *prêt-à-porter* clothing and participating in the major seasonal fashion weeks.

When this was possible, I always ensured on-site access at company headquarters and combined interviews with shadowing at some of these firms. I additionally selected to interview executives in these companies based on the type of influence that was exerted by their formal position. Over a decade ago, Mora (2006, pp. 339–340) had outlined that three types of influence within fashion companies—strategic, technical, and positional—shaped the dominant rhetoric in a fashion firm on managing the relationship between formal structure and everyday work. Strategic influence was obviously exerted by managerial roles. Technical influence would be exhibited by roles with specific know-how, such as visual merchandisers, or the CIO at *MilanModa1*. Positional influence was exerted by transversal functions—such as the VP of Global Marketing at *BritModa*—whose role, in some instances, could directly influence aspects of the design of a fashion collection.

I selected across these roles and preferred gaining access to executive functions that exposed the characteristic duality between aesthetics and business in fashion companies. Alongside executives with strategic influence in long-standing material practice, such as Retail and Communications, newly established positions with technical and positional expertize in e-commerce and online marketing were also selected. For example, alongside the technically influential Director of Media at *BritModa*, I interviewed the Head of Global Supply-Chain—a strategically influential role, founded since the inception of brick-and-mortar operations in the company. This was a sound strategy. The micro-sociological approach in selecting across influential roles, when it was possible to obtain access to such interviews, helped explain how creative executives representing formal structure and areas of influence other than design, approached the production of new practice. Challenged to function on a new digital channel that required designing practices with tangible commercial significance, executives representing different parts of the organizational structure in *MilanModa1*, *MilanModa2*, *MilanModa3*, *Maison Française*, and *BritModa*, unmistakably exhibited different emotion-laden responses: "indifference", "fear", or "excitement". Both new and established executives revealed this sensitivity to answering challenging questions, as they navigated their novel or amended roles in the formal structure. The approach solidified the validity of Burawoy's advice to sample stimulating social situations, rather than populations, when exposing and interpreting data that were extremely difficult to capture otherwise.

One example which speaks to the soundness of Burawoy's (1998) hypothesis and epitomizes the emotional response of high-fashion executives, who listened very little to digital entrepreneurs, and a lot to their digitally distressed peers, was garnered by me at a luxury fashion conference in late 2011. At a heated discussion on luxury fashion and e-commerce in London, poker-faced fashion executives were breaking down one by one, as a well-known fashion consultant harangued at the top of the gathering: "before the Internet, the brands survived, because they were *different...* Now, it's a jungle! When you search for Rolex, it's a Jungle! No, *we* have our own rules as luxury!" By "jungle", the consultant was referring to the ostensible lack of organizing logic in Google-generated search results, appearing after an online user entered a search phrase. The debate I witnessed during a breakout session on technology, briefly discussed below, shows how basic concepts, such as Search Engine Optimization (SEO), were fundamentally foreign, yet universally feared by, new e-commerce hires in fashion companies. Simply put, knowing SEO made it possible for fashion firms to be "found" in the aforementioned "jungle" by optimizing their content for search by keyword on the largest search engines.

At the time, there existed few fashion consultants in brick-and-mortar fashion, who agreed that there may be a new paradigm emerging out of the digital channel for fashion companies, which was to be co-created through trial and error with the help of new companies in digital fashion that were born online and had already initiated this transition to new sources of value for the industry. As a matter of fact, such an argument could be considered a little more than offensive, at the time. Yet, luxury fashion executives from world-renowned brands attended the conference, walking around dazed and frustrated. These delegates from elite institutions found it difficult to understand how or why to persuade their boards of directors to invest in digital practice. At the breakout session, a Senior Project Manager for e-commerce at a large fashion conglomerate kept asking colleagues how to respond to executive management's concerns regarding the "relevancy of new digital tools and practice to the needs of 250-year-old brands". An e-commerce Director at a UK luxury fashion brand indicated that despite the hiring of SEO and social media staff in her team, she was (as we established was common) separated from the "Head of Digital", tripling the time it took new hires to respond to a problem. "If the question is not specific enough, you have to brainstorm it with yourself", she exhaled with palpable frustration. "Once you have the information you want, it's too late. We all know that digital is too fast, and you cannot miss a step. You really have to have someone to work on the specific brand, even if from group level. We probably need 15 - 16 persons in the team. Yes, you can touch the brand; yes, you can educate about the brand. But, I think we need someone who is really like an editor, and gives a different voice [...] someone needs to be hired to bring the level of the conversation on a whole other level".

The Director of *Partner Division* at *Digital Moda*, whom I had just met, was in charge of this particular, prolonged and agonizing, discussion. He was confident and strategic, patient and practical, when handling the various concerns of round-table participants. His first order of business was to explain e-commerce and SEO to fashion executives before him. His advice was actual and his approach was straightforward. He seemed to advocate that fashion brands could, in fact, engage in Internet activities on their own, provided that they followed the existing contextual consensus imparted by online-born "insiders" (such as *Digital Moda*), who knew the business of fashion online. The implication was that to succeed online, fashion brands had to either be hard at work in learning about e-commerce and social commerce, or collaborate with qualitatively new type of legitimating partners.

> Do you have metrics behind your business?" the *Partner Division* Director asked casually, interrupting the discussion of fashion company attendees in the session on how best to approach senior executives in their respective firms for financial help with e-commerce. His audience was stymied, expressions of apprehension on their faces. "When you look at sales, you can't really say, I spent one per cent and one per cent came back", he continued. "But when you see the trend in sales, it should be at least the starting point for you to ask for more money from your board of directors". "How *do* you run SEO campaigns?" asked one fashion executive. The Director of *Partner Division* turned around, facing the questioner, and countered: "Can I ask you, what *do* you mean by SEO?" Unsure, the expert responded, "Search engine optimization...?" *Digital Moda*'s executive was persistent: "No, no ... I mean, you pay a digital agency to do *what exactly?*" The manager offered confusedly, "We pay an agency to do our web marketing and social media for us. They are testing," he mumbled, "... moving keywords, I guess.

It took some persistence for the *Partner Division* Director to negotiate a simplified, clear picture for the fashion community at the table. "We're talking about a search engine, Google. Google needs content and this content has to be relevant. The SEO expert—she or he does what? Changes the content? Moves keywords around? *This doesn't make a lot of sense.* About SEO: Once you've done it; you've done it. You have to optimize your system so that it produces intelligent URLs. *Period.* Names. Category. Product. *Period.* Then, you need text on your site, and the text needs to be seen by search engines. *When this is done, you don't need an SEO expert at all.*" Everyone was scribbling on tablets or paper, impressed by the simplicity (and free-of-charge offer!) of this advice. This subtle decision to disavow directional control was a legitimating narrative well played. It was precisely this degree of creative persuasion that motivated eventually most of the incumbents at that table to respond to novelty, and for a selected few, to partnership with *Digital Moda.*

BIBLIOGRAPHY

Aspers, P., & Godart, F. (2013). Sociology of fashion: Order & change. *Annual Review of Sociology, 39,* 171–192.

Blumer, H. (1969). Fashion: From class differentiation to collective selection. *The Sociological Quarterly, 10*(3), 275–291.

Bourdieu, P., & Delsaut, Y. (1975). Le couturier et sa griffe: Contribution à une théorie de la magie. *Actes de la Recherche en Sciences Sociales, 1*(1), 7–36.

Burawoy, M. (1998). The extended case method. *Sociological Theory, 16*(1), 4–33.

Crane, D. (2012). *Fashion and its social agendas: Class, gender, and identity in clothing.* Chicago: University of Chicago Press.

Davis, F. (1992). *Fashion, culture, and identity.* Chicago: University of Chicago Press.

Entwistle, J., & Rocamora, A. (2006). The field of fashion materialized: A study of London fashion week. *Sociology, 40*(4), 735–751.

Garud, R., & Karnøe, P. (2003). Bricolage versus breakthrough: Distributed and embedded agency in technology entrepreneurship. *Research Policy, 32*(2), 277–300.

Hebdige, D. (1979). *Subculture: The meaning of style.* London: Routledge.

March, J.G., Sproull, L.S., & Tamuz, M. (1991). Learning from samples of one or fewer. *Organization Science, 2*(1), 1–13.

Mora, E. (2006). Collective production of creativity in the Italian fashion system. *Poetics, 34*(6), 334–353.

Shah, S.K., & Tripsas, M. (2007). The accidental entrepreneur: The emergent and collective process of user entrepreneurship. *Strategic Entrepreneurship Journal, 1*(1–2), 123–140.

Simmel, G. (1957). Fashion. *American Journal of Sociology, 62*(6), 541–558.

Vedres, B., & Stark, D. (2010). Structural folds, generative disruption in overlapping groups. *American Journal of Sociology, 115*(4), 1150–1190.

von Hippel, E. (1994). 'Sticky information' and the locus of problem solving: Implications for innovation. *Management Science, 40*(4), 429–439.

INDEX

© The Editor(s) (if applicable) and The Author(s) 2018
I. Petkova, *Engineering Legitimacy*,
https://doi.org/10.1007/978-3-319-90707-9

187